Zek

The Convict

By
Artem Vaskanyan

Cadmus Publishing
www.cadmuspublishing.com

Copyright © 2022 Artem Vaskanyan

Published by Cadmus Publishing
www.cadmuspublishing.com
Port Angeles, WA

ISBN: 978-1-63751-156-5

All rights reserved. Copyright under Berne Copyright Convention, Universal Copyright Convention, and Pan-American Copyright Convention. No part of this book may be reproduced, stored in a retrieval system, or transmitted in any form, or by any means, electronic, mechanical, photocopying, recording or otherwise, without prior permission of the author.

ABOUT THE AUTHOR

Ever since I was young, I wanted to learn how to write, but I could never attend school like a normal kid since my family always moved from place to place like some gypsies in a caravan. Such nomadic life made it impossible for me to stay in school and pursue my dream as a writer.

I'm originally from southwest Asia, Baku, Azerbaijan, a place that is well-known for black caviar and oil fields. My life there was peaceful and happy; however, at age seven all of that changed when my family and I suddenly had to flee the country for our lives when the war between Armenia and Azerbaijan broke out over disputed land; and since we were Armenians and Christians, staying in a Muslim country was no longer safe. Before I could finish the first grade, I found myself on the train traveling north to the Russian parts of the Soviet Union.

Living in my new home was not easy since we continued to move from one province, town, city to another every few months and at times even weeks, preventing me staying in school and adapting to my new home. Eventually, my family and I came to the United States in 1993 from Moscow, Russia with an Armenian Refugee status. I was only 13.

When I went to middle school to eighth grade, I found it to be extremely challenging since not only was I not able to speak the language, but my level of education was of a second grader; and being suddenly exposed to a completely different culture and traditions made it even more difficult to acclimatize to the new environment that I would reluctantly force myself to call my new home.

Ever since I left my home my life has never been the same, and it didn't even matter where I lived, whether it was in Russia or in the United States, it was always nomadic.

For the seven years that I managed to live "free" in the U.S. prior to being incarcerated, my lifestyle did not change for the better. As a matter of fact, it even became worse. At first, I didn't understand why I was always angry at life and agitated with everyone; and when I ostracized myself from everyone, I found relief by turning to drugs and alcohol, followed by criminal acts. Not long after that I was incarcerated at age 20, and it was there in complete loneliness, abandonment, and despair that I was able to tap into my inner self and discover that the reason for my self-destructive behaviors was because of my severe depression that continued to stay with me since I was a young kid where I often wished to be somewhere else and someone else.

In Memory of My Father
Artem Vaskanyan
(1936-1979)

Contents

- Day I: A Call 1
- Day I: Rendezvous 5
- Day I: The Entrance 9
- Day I: Master Yourself 13
- Day I: Behind the Prison Walls 22
- Day II: The Cloud 30
- Day II: Love 36
- Day II: Suffering 41
- Day II: Beast On a Chain 47
- Day III: Life and Death 53
- Day III: Pure Mind 60
- Day III: Understanding 70
- Day III: Virtuoso Vor (Thief) 78
- Day IV: The Crossing 83
- Day IV: Four Noble Truths 86
- Day IV: Between Two Realms 92
- Day IV: The Noble Eightfold Path 95
- Day IV: Errant Mind 102
- Day V: Great Doubt 108
- Day V: An Angry Wasp 112
- Day V: Eradicating Negativity 117
- Day V: Two Kinds 121
- Day V: Inferno 125
- Day VI: The Path to Buddhahood 134
- Day VI: The Lonely Path 139
- Day VI: Vagabond 143
- Day VI: The Middle Path 150
- Day VI: That Place 153
- Day VI: Nonviolent Way 156
- Day VI: True Practice 162
- Day VI: Two Waters 164
- Day VI: Betrayal 167
- Day VI: The Key 172
- Day VII: Zen 177
- Day VII: A Fallen Fruit 181
- Day VII: The Ways of Our Ancestors 184
- Day VII: Small Creatures 189
- Day VII: The Mind 201
- Day VII: Last Supper 205
- Day VII: Patience 209
- Day VII: The Way of the Spirit 213
- Day VIII: Departure 217

Day 1
A Call

I like to think of myself as a poet
Who has spent half of his life
In maximum security prisons,
And not as *zek* (a prisoner/convict).
I like to think that I've managed
To preserve my humanity intact,
Despite all the hardships that I've endured.
I like to think of myself as a good man,
Although I've done many wrongs,
And perhaps by doing some good in my life,
I can change the course of my karmic actions,
And hopefully find myself on the path
To enlightenment.

I think it was somewhere at the end of summer, or more like at the beginning of autumn to be exact; but I remember clearly on that day there was a storm brewing, and the dark clouds were growing larger by the minute over the city; and I hadn't seen any sunlight for a whole week. I was starting to believe that I might never have a chance to see it in my lifetime again.

I felt hopeless and lonely. This wasn't what I anticipated to have instilled for me in life, especially not after I was released *iz tyur'mí* (from prison) where I've spent all my twenties and thirties. Where I was waiting and hoping and praying at the most desperate times to get a second chance in life to be free; and now that I have finally attained it, I don't feel all that impressed by it.

That sunless day, I had no work and nowhere to go to enjoy myself. I found myself daydreaming throughout the day and then falling asleep in hopes that I would be awakened by someone or something to bring me some kind of joy into my lonely, desolate life. Perhaps an experience of some sort that would make me feel alive again and drag me out of this melancholic state of mind.

Of course, I had many darker days such as this before, especially throughout those long, lonely years that I endured v *tyur'mé* (in prison), but somehow, I've always managed to get back on my feet no matter how gloomy my situation would appear to be. And yet, this feeling of hopelessness, I couldn't shake it off. It just wouldn't leave me alone since being released three months ago to this very day.

I guess I feel more disillusioned with the freedom that I so impatiently craved for more than anything else in *mayéyi zhízni* (my life).

I'm embarrassed to admit, but there were moments in my confined life when I felt freer, happier, and even more alive than I do now in this so-called free world. Nevertheless, for some mysterious reason I still believe with what's left of *mayéyi dushe* (my soul) that today will be the day where a new beginning is underway.

The next thing I knew, it was a phone call out of the blue that late afternoon from *diadia* (uncle) Y*ú*ra on my mother's side.

I was thrilled to hear his deeply missed voice that instantly put a smile on my face as soon as I heard it, and it made me remember that I could be easily amused when I talk to the right person. And I was even more surprised when I found out that he just became anointed as a Buddhist *Zen* Monk at the Forest Monastery; and even more excited when he invited me to come and join him at the monastery for a seven-day retreat known as *sesshin* in Zen practice.

I was elated like I had just been promoted to head chef at the *Bon-Jórno* Restaurante where I worked as a janitor and a dishwasher since I've been out. I wanted to scream, laugh out loud, and jump on top of the kitchen table and tap dance with pure joy, but I thought twice before I made any noise in my tiny, one bedroom apartment since my neighbors love to call *mentám* (cops) every time they hear a slight noise, especially in my case, an *ex-zek* (an ex-con) disturbing the peace, that might be just enough to violate my probation and get me thrown back in *tyur'mú* (prison). So, I held my inner joy without a peep and danced and laughed instead inside *mayéyi dushé* (my soul) with all my heart and joy.

I gladly had agreed with several da! (yes!), responding joyously to my *díadía* Yúra, and as I hung up the phone I instantly packed my Army bag and headed to the bus station to catch the ride to the Forest Zen Monastery.

On the bus I found a comfortable seat in the corner back away from the rest of the passengers and their loud conversations. One thing that never changes about people whether they are inside or outside the prison walls is that they always find a way to make noise. That is one human nature that will never change in all men.

I put my headphones on and turned the music on to Ivan Kuchin, the Russian singer, and dozed off to his lyrics of prison walls, survival, and love of life as the bus drove away from the brewing storm, the dark clouds that were circling above my head, and from the loneliness and melancholy that was draining every drop of life that was left in me.

It is crazy how life is!
One minute I'm in a state of total desolation;
But then the next, I'm happy!
It is crazy how a simple phone call has a power
To change my life from gloom to happiness;
And even though I don't know for sure what's waiting
For me on the other side, I can feel it in my gut

That it will be much better than what is left for me
Back in the city
It is crazy how life is!
For it only took a call to rejuvenate me.

Day I
Rendezvous

The ride was smooth, it was only an hour long, but during that hour my anticipation for the seven-day retreat was building up, and my appetite for a new life experience was growing stronger with every mile. I'll finally have a chance to experience the Buddhist practice in a real Buddhist Monastery surrounded by the true, genuine Buddhist Monks and practitioners, one of whom is my *díadía* (uncle) Yúra.

I arrived at my destination surrounded by the forest in leaves, and as I got off the bus, I felt a tingling sensation all over my body. I was excited to meet my uncle, who I hadn't seen for years. I stepped off the bus with an electrifying smile on my face and feeling the weight of loneliness coming off my shoulders. I looked around, straining my eyes to see if my *diadía* was already waiting for me, but he was nowhere to be found.

The bus drove off, leaving me behind in the dust standing alone in the middle of the road between two forests. I stood and looked for my *diadía* in all directions; and as I was about to lose all hope, I saw a familiar figure of an older man appearing out of the forest's thick woods heading my way with an electrifying smile on his face resembling mine.

At last, it was my *Diadía Yúra* coming to meet me. He no longer had that hippie-like curly, long hair coming down his shoulders. His pornstache that I made fun of all the time and his bushy eyebrows were all cleanly shaven to the last blade of hair. His flashy clothes and jewelry that he loved to wear so much were all replaced with a brown monk's robe and prayer beads wrapped around his wrist, representing humility and rebirth into a new life.

"*Zdaróva! Diadía* Yúra (Hello! Uncle Yúra). I can't believe my eyes!" I said and reached out for a hug.

"You're not the only one who is surprised. Look at how big and strong you've grown," tapping on the back of my shoulders, smiling as we hugged.

"*Slúshayi Diadía* (Listen, uncle), I have to ask, what the hell! What made you decide to become a monk?"

"*Eto dólgaya istóriya* (It's a long story). I can't explain it with a few words, but you'll understand during *sesshin*, the seven-day retreat, and even maybe you'll become a monk yourself?"

"Ha! Don't hold your breath! If I haven't become one after so many damn years while being locked up like *sabáka* (a dog), I highly doubt that I ever will. Besides, I have practically lived as one without good food, women, comfortable clothes, and soft bed for too damn long; but I am hopeful that this retreat will guide me to the right path *v zhízni* (in life), for I feel lost and angry at life."

"Unfortunately, everything you said is true and you have every right to feel the way you do. You've spent too many years in inhumane places since you were young. *Prastí minyá* (Forgive me) that I couldn't come to see you as often as I should've." He said with a sad face and watery eyes. "But let's not talk of the past. Let's talk about today. Since this experience will help you to heal the wounds, and most importantly, guide you to the right path that you've been so desperately searching for; and I promise you that for as long as you'll practice *s atkrítam sérdzam* (with an open heart), you will find it," he said.

"I'll try my best, and *spasíba* (thanks) for the invite," I responded, and then we both walked into the heart of the forest from where he came out.

We walked in complete silence up a narrow alley between the forest trees as there was nothing else to say to each other after 20 years of barely seeing and talking to one another. The truth was that there was too much to say, I just didn't know how to say it, and I feel that that's exactly how he felt too.

I followed his footprints in the grass that he left behind, and I just couldn't help myself but to ponder how much we both had changed. He no longer was that same *díadía* (uncle) for whom I've stole and with whom I occasionally smoked ganjas, drank vodka, partied at the night clubs from sunset to sunrise, and picked fights with men twice my size, all to build my courage and toughness like he was preparing me for a hard life. But now I am looking at a different man, a humble monk full of composure, and a complete opposite of a man I once—what seemed to be like yesterday—knew. I felt like we were complete strangers who just met for the first time.

I remember him always talking. Coming up with all sorts of comical stories. Always entertaining, always laughing and joking, and always surrounded by *krasívami zhénshinami* (beautiful women). He used to love to show off his new clothes and jewelry that I used to steal for him. And every time when I would see him, he would have something new on. Always looking elegant, chic to the point that when he would enter into the room, he would catch everyone's attention; and I always tried to be just like him. Even now he continues to amaze me with his new look. Even this brown robe looks like a suit on him. Becoming a monk at age 65 is a hell of a change. What kind of person does that? Of course, I too have changed, perhaps even more than he did. Or on second thought, maybe not as much, but I did, only in a different way, since for the past 20 years I was full of despair, loneliness, and always felt like I was living on the edge. But then again, I could be wrong since my *díadía* Yúra was once *Vor V Zakóne* (Thief-In-Law, or in other words, *zek* (a convict) who dedicates his life to the criminal life) while being a part of the *Rúskayi organizóvaniyi prestúpnosti* (Russian organized crime) since he was a young man when he lived back in the Soviet Union and in the United States while I was still locked up; but I don't exactly know for sure to tell the truth, the lifestyle that he led during my lingering absence, but I think that it would be fair to say that we both have changed most drastically in our own ways. But I'm just glad that both of our paths that are so unique in their own way and in many ways are so much alike, have found themselves somehow to cross once again.

My mind was racing with uncontrollable thoughts as I was trying to come up with a reasonable explanation for what made my *díadía* choose to live a life in complete seclusion. And not by force, like it was done to me, but out of his own volition. I know of loneliness all too well. I know that it can bring you peace, but it can also ruin you just as well. Nevertheless, these questions flooded my mind relentlessly, in the end leaving me with two goals to pursue: to put myself on the right path; and the other to find out the true reason that caused my *díadía* to choose such an isolated way to live his life. Perhaps if I was to understand what made him become a monk, I may then discover the way I can find internal peace for myself. For God knows, I've tried like hell, but all I found in the end was more pain.

I was so baffled by all of these intriguing questions that I completely missed the beautiful scenes of nature as we walked in silence through the forest. I must admit that I was silent on the outside, but full of noise on the inside, like a brewing storm that I thought I had left behind. Before I knew it, I saw the Buddhist Zen Monastery with the pagoda roof standing erect like a giant dragon on its heels.

Day 1
The Entrance

The forest monastery stood on top of the hill at the precipice with cobblestone stairs leading up to a large wooden gateway entrance into the monastery. At the entrance I was greeted by a heavy-set monk who stood by the gate, welcoming me with a low bow and a smile. His face was plump with a huge mouth and thick lips. He handed me a grey robe to wear, prepared for new practitioners. I changed inside a small cabin by the gateway and was asked to leave behind all of my belongings. None of the material possessions were allowed to be carried inside the monastery. Anything that would remind a practitioner of the materialistic world must all be abandoned during *sesshin*.

"For the first few days of the retreat a person's mind will be attached to the place where he came from and crave for his belongings. By separating a practitioner from his possessions will improve the clarity of his mind," said my *diadía* (uncle). I hesitated for a moment, wondering if I was in fact in the right place that would help me to change my life around and that I wasn't putting myself through the same process like it was done to me in prison where everything from me was taken on the first moment of my arrival.

"For the entire seven days starting today, that life you know outside the monastery cannot be part of you. When *sesshin* ends, you'll understand the reason for such strict rules. Everything will make sense then. *Pavér' mnye!* (Trust me!)" my *diadía* said, smiling and placing his hand on my shoulder for a moment, then leaving me with another monk as he went inside the housing without saying another word. I guess one thing that didn't change about him was that he would come and go when it suited him. It was always his way or the highway. To be frank, I was kind of glad to see that part of him come out for I do miss his old self.

I waited by the entrance dressed in my new outfit as the new arrivals such as myself began to arrive for the seven-day retreat. It wasn't long until all of us, maybe around 20 or so, were gathered by the cabin dressed as Buddhist Zen practitioners in brown robes. We then were met by the large monk with wide shoulders who walked with a limp to escort us inside the dwelling place to our rooms.

On the way into the housing, I noticed up in the dark-blue sky a raven circling above the pagoda's rooftop searching for prey. Somehow, I felt connected to the raven, for he and I weren't too different. For starters, both of us were searching, he for the prey to strike and feed upon, and I for a meaningful life experience that I could learn from and fill an empty void in my heart. Both of our lives essentially depended on what we find. He cannot survive without his prey, and I cannot survive without my purpose in life. In either case, we both possessed a great desire to search relentlessly until we find what our heart desires.

I walked at the end of a single file following my fellow practitioners through hallways as wide as my arms full-length stretched out, passing rooms that we were assigned to as we entered them one by one. By the side of every room's door candles were lit along the wooden walls; and on the opposite side of each door small square windows were half open, blowing a gentle breeze from the outside garden and causing the candles' light to dance and dwindle.

I walked until the monk and I were the only ones left walking in the empty hallway when he abruptly stopped and opened the door to my room in the middle of the hallway. I thanked him silently with a head nod as I entered. He nodded back and closed the door behind me. That was weirdly uncomfortable, I thought to myself. It wasn't so much for the silence but for being with an unfamiliar person in the middle of the hallway alone.

The room was as I expected, extremely plain. A bed with a pillow placed on top. In the corner of the room and by the bed's side was a small bureau with a lit candle set on top of it, and directly above the bed was an open window as wide as the width of my shoulders with a view of a sunset in the far horizon.

The room was cozy despite the fact that there was nothing entertaining in it but me and the lit candle. We were the only two essences of life that radiated warmth and energy inside the room. Nevertheless, it reminded me of the many prison cells that I was in except for a large open window that I always dreamed to have, and how can I forget the barred iron door and toilet and sink right next to my bunk. For years my *klétka* (cell) was my bedroom, living room, dining room, bathroom, entertainment room. It was my kitchen, laundry, gym, library, my temple, and it would become a place of whatever I wanted it to be when I converted the six-by-nine-foot cell into what I needed; and instead of a mattress, I always had to use two wool blankets that I would fold several times with cardboard inserted in between them for sturdiness. I could never lay down, never mind fall asleep, on the prison mattress. It was like sleeping on rocks.

I adjusted the sleeves of my new clothes. It was a perfect fit, something that I didn't realize earlier when I was getting dressed and was overwhelmed from leaving my belongings behind. Wearing my new clothes, I must admit, felt awkwardly soothing and even pleasant. I never expected the monk's robe to be so comfortable. For 20 years all I was allowed to wear was the grey abrasive prison uniforms outside my *klétki* (cell). However, inside my *klétki* I always wore just boxers. I could never get used to wearing those prison clothes. It was like wearing a jumpsuit.

I laid awake with eyes wide open, looking at the window across from me with a beautiful view of a full red-yellow moon appearing with a glow and smiling back at me. I felt hypnotized by its increasing glow and unwillingly found myself gently shutting my eyes for only a brief moment.

I stepped into the other side
through the entrance gate that was already open.
The sweet-smelling lilac shrubs with the large clusters
of violet, greyish-pink, some purple, and some
white flowers were everywhere I looked.
I was home!
In one of my *favor*ed out of many unhappy places
where I grew up.
I picked a violet flower from the shrub
and held it delicately on my open palm.
The flower looked too gentle, too innocent, too pure,
I could never relate to her
not even to her single leaflet.
For my soul had been wounded too deeply by life, and
only a soul as damaged as mine has the power to heal me.

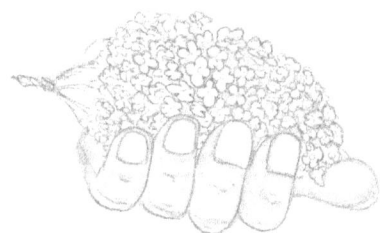

Day 1
Master Yourself

What felt like a brief moment was actually an hour, as I was awakened by the loud, repeating sounds of the gong. I stepped out of my room and saw practitioners walking down the hallway. I followed them until we reached *zendo*, a large meditation hall set up with *zaffus* meditation pillows in a rectangular shape. At the entrance, a thin looking monk who looked like he hadn't eaten in a few days very politely told us to take our sandals off and then bow prior to entering. It was just like entering into the dojo where at the entrance I had to take my shoe-wear off and bow, and everyone who would notice me would greet me with a bow in return. It gave me a feeling of déjà vu and I felt a sense of belonging in a place that was so pleasantly known and at the same time so enigmatic to me.

On the way to my seat, I bowed to the enormous bronze Buddha statue that was at least 10 times the size of an ordinary man. The Buddha was calmly seated in a full lotus inside the stupa that was richly decorated with various colorful flowers, offerings made by the Buddhist monks and visitors. On the Buddha's chest there was a swastika, a symbol in a form of a cross with four arms of equal length bent at right angles clockwise, and as I later came to find out that the Buddha was not a member of the Nazi party, but that it was ancient symbol since prehistoric times representing the cycle of life, death, and rebirth, as well as good fortune and protection against the evil spirits.

I then bowed to the *roshi*, the Japanese Zen Master, who was sitting in a full lotus just like the Buddha behind him. He was a tall, skinny old man, I imagine about 70 or so, whose wrinkled face showed nothing but kindness and his commitment to the Zen practice. Above the *roshi* and to the left side of the Buddha statue was a short, heavyset young monk with a long nose that made his clean-shaven face appear unattractive. He was striking with the padded mallet in the center of a rimmed, round, bronze disk with a heavy set of blows producing loud, sonorous sounds that only moments ago woke me up.

I then proceeded to take a seat on the *zaffu* at the end of the hall in a half lotus, just like others around me had; and as I sat, I couldn't help but to examine everything that I laid my eyes on, and as I looked around, I began to imitate the full lotus posture from the Buddha statue by pulling with difficulty my other foot further from the half lotus towards my hip. Thanks to my on and off karate training since my childhood years it still allowed me to stay flexible and in good physical shape. By observing *roshi*, I sat up straight, shoulders back, head forward; and by watching the monks around me, I lowered my gaze to a few feet in front of me and brought my hands together, placing them at the level of my navel.

As the new and old practitioners continued to enter the meditation hall to take seats, it became obvious who were the pupils amongst them and who were the lifelong practitioners. The amateurs, such as myself, were like kids at the zoo, looking at everything with their piercing gazes and open mouths in awe, in contrast to the old practitioners who were silent and calm like a motionless sea.

Two young ladies in their late 20s appeared on my left. The brunette affectionately smiled at me and then bowed as she sat down next to me. Her chin slightly trembled as she coughed and her pretty nose snuffled. She looked nervous from being in the crowded room, and I noticed how she perspired on her forehead as her big brown eyes ignited with eagerness and excitement and raced to all directions as they playfully jumped from one corner of the hall to the other. From one monk's shiny bald head to another. Her body twisted and turned in all directions like a worm you hold at the tips of your fingers and thumb before you pierce it on the fishing hook. The redhead seated next to her appeared to be distracted like she would rather be somewhere else but here; but then she managed to regain her concentration by taking a few deep breaths in and out and then sat motionless, staring with her piercing gaze at the Buddha, devouring him with her eyes. It was obvious that one of them seemed to be more experienced than the other.

Minutes later they both began to smile as their eyes became more relaxed and the brunette's zippy movements came to a halt. I was just like them, fascinated by what I saw and overwhelmed with pure joy just to be a part of this new experience. However, I expressed my joy on the inside, while on the outside I remained rooted to the spot as the Buddha statue. Although it was all new to me, I was yet able to quickly find my niche and appear to the beginners as if I was a long-time practitioner. It was something that I became good at, hiding my true feelings from others. It is one of the qualities that all *zéki* (convicts) learn in prison which is to never show your true emotions. No matter how good or bad the day gets, never let other cons know your weaknesses and strengths. After all, *zek* (a convict) has only one enemy *v tyur'mé* (in prison) and that is another *zek* since it is another *zek* that betrays, manipulates, and steals from another.

My posture looked like I knew what I was doing and in a way I did, since I have practiced yoga for some years. I got into practicing yoga when I sustained an injury in my lower back from overtraining, and ever since I started practicing it, I fell in love with it and never stopped. For me yoga became the way of life as I religiously stretched my body before and after my workouts. However, I was no expert, and I have to stress on that since many people assume right away that every yoga practitioner can put his foot behind his head or stand on his head for hours. That is a false assumption that I often found myself faced with when people would see me stretching in the gym. When I say to people that I'm practicing yoga, right away they want you to turn into a pretzel. That is frustrating and even offensive. And although I practice yoga, I hate meditating. It is just too boring.

The *zendo* was now full. All of the *zaffus* were taken by the old and new practitioners and monks. *roshi* was observing attentively the flock of practitioners in front of him. He cleared his throat with several loud coughs into his closed hand, preparing to speak. Then he reached for a small wooden mallet and struck the small metal bell shaped as a bowl three times.

Ding!... Ding!... Ding!...

The sound of euphony resonated throughout the hall bringing composure, calm, peace, followed by dead silence as the sounds of coughs, sniffs, and movements faded into the background.

"Namaste! Welcome all to the *sesshin*, the seven-day retreat," he said with his palms held together vertically in front of his chest as he bowed.

"Namaste!" we all simultaneously responded and bowed back.

"Today we'll discuss and practice meditation techniques that we'll continue to work on to improve throughout the *sesshin*. Okay! So, let's begin by sitting comfortably on the *zaffu*. You may sit in half lotus position or if your knees bother you then you may simply take a seat in the chair in the back, and if they do not, then you may sit in a full lotus like this." (He bent his other foot over and placed it on his thigh).

The two young ladies on my left adjusted their *zaffus* simultaneously and looked at each other with a satisfying look. The brunette leaned toward the redhead and whispered into her ear.

"Wow! I can't believe this guy (referring to me) is sitting in a full lotus. He must be an expert!" As she sat back, I noticed in my peripheral vision a gayly smile appeared on her face. At that point my ego took over and I ignored the pain that was beginning to arise in both of my knees, and yet, I didn't budge a muscle nor act like I felt a single pinch of pain. Instead, I only lifted my head slightly higher out of pride. Part of me felt ashamed, pretending to be someone I was not just because I wanted to look good; and yet, I still refused to budge as my ego stood its ground.

"Straighten your backs, shoulders pushed back slightly to open up your chest. Lower your gaze to three feet in front of you. Pick a spot and concentrate on it. Relax your eyes, a soft gaze. You may choose to meditate with your eyes closed, but then you would have to try harder to stay awake, to stay in the present moment. In either case, focus on your breathing, let your breath guide you throughout your meditation. You may place your hands on top of your knees or on top of each other in front of you like this…" (He demonstrated to the group how to properly place the hands during meditation and placed the back of one hand on top an open palm of another and pressed them close under his navel.)

    I looked down on both of my hands and adjusted them to what *roshi* advised by placing them closer to my navel. As I was about to switch from the full lotus position into the half lotus, I caught a glimpse of the brunette looking at me attentively, imitating me to the last detail. My ego took over once again and I remained still with increasing pain in both my knees. I felt like there were nails inserted into my kneecaps. I took a deep breath in and slowly exhaled to relieve some of the torment, and as I did so, I heard both of the ladies exhale right after me. My narcissistic pride grew larger with every drop of glance that was laid upon me, inflating my chest like a balloon. I remained motionless and felt numb to my self-inflicted agony.

    "Breathing is everything! If you don't breathe correctly then you cannot get the full experience out of meditation. So, let's try this exercise. Take a few deep breaths in and out." He gestured with his hand to begin. (Everyone inhaled and slowly exhaled.)

    "Excellent! Now, inhale halfway and hold your breath in for 30 seconds; and then, inhale short breaths and push the air down, sending and pressing the breaths of air two inches below your navel, one after another. Then press and hold the air by inhaling more of the short breaths, and exhale in small amounts of air as you are about to inhale again; and hold for 30 seconds or within your comfort zone." (Everyone was inhaling then gasping for air, then exhaling and inhaling again.)

    "And now, slowly exhale every last drop of air that you hold from the bottom of your lungs and then breathe normally." (Everyone exhaled slowly.)

    "Okay! Since everyone is doing so well, I think we are ready for meditation. So, let's meditate for a little bit!" *roshi* said joyfully and reached for a *jukpi*, a wooden stick used for meditation sessions, and smacked it on his open palm twice, the signal to begin.

For the first few minutes the ladies and I were breathing as one. Every time I would inhale or exhale, adjust my back, shoulders, or arms, I would see them do the same.

Twenty minutes had passed. My knees were in so much pain that my right eye began to twitch, and a teardrop appeared and glided down my cheek onto my mustache and then slid down into the side of my mouth. The salty taste of my teardrop had brought me back into the present moment of pain, discomfort, and loneliness. It had awakened me from the indulgent fantasies that I found myself becoming infatuated with throughout my meditation. As I looked down at my bare feet, I saw that they were as blue as the morning sky. I wanted to scream from the pain, but instead I bit my bottom lip and held the pain within. I then unlocked my bluish-numb feet from the full lotus and felt the fire rushing through my lifeless legs. I tried to move my toes, but my feet and legs were not with me, they were numb and cold like ice and at the same time on fire. My mind and body were not as one, it felt like they were of two different entities. I sat with my legs outstretched, massaging them with my hands to bring them back to life. The blood began to flow like a river from the top of the mountain and I felt reinvigorated to what I was before, of one mind and flesh.

My mind felt strong and proud from overcoming my egomania, like I had broken the magic seal that kept me locked in my own vainglorious way. My pride dispersed, but then immediately was replaced with another from feeling guilty at not staying seated in full lotus. Will there ever be a way for me to feel true modesty, I pondered.

I glimpsed at the ladies on my left, they were half asleep. Their backs were slanted forward and their heads hung down like heavy, ripened fruits from the stems of the tree. I suppose that their minds had drifted to the realm of fantasies that I myself had just awoken from. I returned to my breathing and began to meditate once again, only this time in half lotus with my eyes slightly open, piercing forward and awake. My body felt tired, but my mind was relaxed and sharp. I remembered *roshi*'s words that he not too long ago said, "Stay in the present, stay awake, and don't drift away." I adapted his words and turned them into a mantra as I began to whisper them breathing out.

I noticed how *roshi* quietly reached for the *jukpi* and grabbed ahold of it, raised it above his head, and with a swift motion of his hand, whacked it on the open palm of his other hand, sending a loud, cracking noise across the *zendo*. The piercing sound of the *jukpi* had awoken all of those whose minds were trapped in the realm of fantasies to the point that some of them jumped off their *zaffu* seats.

"Come back to the present moment! Nothing is more important than being in the here and now!" He placed the *jukpi* to the side and resumed meditation.

When *roshi* had smacked the *jukpi* on the palm of his hand, the two young ladies were caught off guard. The brunette fell off her *zaffu* seat, and the redhead jumped onto her feet. Their faces blushed, embarrassed from being startled to death by the loud, cracking, piercing sound of the *jukpi*.

"This noise had almost blown the socks off my feet!" the brunette whispered to her friend, leaning over to her.

"And it almost blew the wig off my head," the redhead whispered back. They both giggled and smiled in agreement.

The meditation session for that night had ended with *roshi*'s final words. "Don't forget that it takes time and most importantly dedication to the practice to perfect your form and sharpen your mind. Nothing is ever done overnight, but eventually you will become aware of what your form lacks and your mind hungers for, and once you do, adjust, adjust! Adjust to every little change in life in order to succeed. See you all tomorrow morning. *Namaste* and goodnight!" and whacked the *jukpi* twice to end the night.

On the way back to my room I walked like I was crippled, taking one step at a time, dragging one foot after the other, and promising to myself to never again let my pride dominate me. And although my back and knees were hurting from meditating in a full lotus, I will tell you one thing: I am glad that I am not in prison while feeling hurt like this since if I would've tried to get medical help, I would be denied just as quickly as I would ask for it. One thing *v tyur'mé* (in prison) that every *zek* (con) tries to avoid is getting sick or injured since when your health is bad you will never be treated by any of the medical doctors. They will deliberately deny you treatment because of the hate they feel for you.

I remember one time when I injured my lower back from lifting weights. It was so bad that I couldn't even get up from bed the next day. I was like that for months, unable to walk straight or even clean my bowels without shedding tears from my eyes. It really was that bad! I had no other option but to seek medical assistance, which was something that I abhorred to do unless there was no other alternative to my problem. When I saw *vrachá* (a doctor) after a month of waiting to be called and explained to her of my back pain, she would not even prescribe me a single pill of Motrin to help me with my pain. This *bábayagá* (witch) was that evil.

And my case wasn't even that serious in comparison to other prisoners and what they had to go through with prison medical doctors. There were some cases where cons complained for years about their stomachaches and in response were told by prison doctors that they must've ate something bad, but when their pain would escalate to such a level where they would lose consciousness, then they would have to be taken to the outside hospital where they would finally find out after the proper examination by the non-prison medical doctor that they only have weeks left to live because of the stage four colon cancer or the growing tumor. Many *zéki* (convicts) had died while I was *v tyur'mé* and continue to die because of the prison medical doctors who deliberately downplay the seriousness of prisoners' medical conditions. These doctors are committing premeditated murders against *zékav* (prisoners) without ever being punished for their crimes. The animosity towards *zékav* by *tyurémskami vrachámi* (the prison doctors) is so great that it is seen not only by their actions but can also be felt by their evil presence. I know I felt it when I was around them even though I was a nobody, just another *zek* trying to survive amongst the men in the position of power.

In the middle of the hall where my room was, I saw my *díadía* (uncle) mopping the floor gracefully with great pride. I tried to creep up behind him to greet him with surprise.

"Did you master yourself yet?" he asked without turning around before I even had a chance to get closer.

"Not yet! But I most definitely killed both of my knees and hopefully some of my pride along with it."

He slightly smiled and said, "Certain things are not easy to kill, and pride is one of them. However, weaknesses can be overcome, but not until you understand yourself, and to do that you must first master yourself."

When a boxer trains,
His skill improves;
And when he fights for no cause,
He has all his mastery at hand;
But as soon as he begins
To fight for a prize
He panics,
His hands begin to shake,
His knees begin to buckle,
His head spins,
He's short of breath,
He's sweating,
He starts to doubt his skill.
The fear of losing the prize becomes greater
Than losing the fight.
He fights more with himself
Than with his opponent.
He trained to fight against others,
But never against himself.

DAY I
BEHIND THE PRISON WALLS

That night I laid in bed wide awake looking at the full moon through the window in my room and admiring its glowing beauty. I couldn't stop but think of today's experience that only this morning I was back in my apartment, frustrated, depressed, and angry at life. I felt blessed since I'd only been at the monastery not even a full day and I already experienced meditation, Buddhist teachings, and fruitful conversations with a dear *diadía* (uncle) of mine.

I dozed off in deep thought with a gratitude, anxiously looking forward to what tomorrow might bring. I dreamed of my old wretched life, where I saw myself being back in *klétki* (a cage) in a tiny, dark cell looking through the metal bars at the ignorant crowd of people who stood confused outside my cell and pointing their fingers at the cells around me. I slowly approached the barred iron door from the shadows of the corner cell and stood in front of the iron bars, holding them with my hands as I tightened my grip, bringing my forehead against the bars with rage in my eyes as they turned bright red. Angry, not from being in the cell, but from being surrounded by the ignorant who don't even try to understand what prison does to a young man. I yelled out to them…

You don't know!
What a man goes through behind the prison walls
A man behind the prison walls
Wakes up to the sound of whistles and screams by guards
Instead of the sounds of a crowing rooster at the farm
As he often dreams to have.
He's counted like a sheep at the farm and fed like a stock;
And told by guards when he can see his family,
Make a phone call, eat, sleep, wake up, or
Make movement of any kind.
What he can read, write, draw, watch, say, and listen to;
His every move is being watched, controlled to such degree
That every positive thought or idea is discouraged.
He's forced to believe
That he's a failure and a disgrace
As he's looked upon with scrutiny and doubt
At everything he touches,
All his achievements and successes can't be shared
With whom he wishes;
And every person that lives with him throughout
The day and night
Is a potential enemy to face at any given moment
During his life.
He's treated worse than a dog
For as long as he remains confined,
And if he doesn't protest such inhumane treatment,
Then he will make himself forget
What being human is all about.
This degradation tears him down
It makes him feel less human than he is,

A failure and a mistake.
He starts to lose all hope in all humanity
And at any chance to have a normal life someday.
It's their job to tear him down like a wall,
But never to build him back up,
That's left entirely upon him to do with bitterness,
Anger, and rage that has built up in his heart
From the long process of confinement and neglect.
If you haven't been
Where a man behind the prison walls has been,
Or seen what he has seen,
Then you wouldn't understand the hidden message in the dream
That I reveal.
I pray to God!
That no man will ever have such days
That many men behind the prison walls have.
I wouldn't wish this kind of life
On my worst enemy.
Because a prison isn't a place for any man
Who has a soul.
It's a soulless place that will drain
Anyone's life away without pity.
If you truly wish to understand
What a man behind the prison walls is going through
Then dig deep down into the heart of your soul
Like you have never dug before,
And find the most repugnant,
Most shameful dark secret in your life,
Your worst mistake,
That just a simple thought of it
Will rip your heart out of your chest,
Bring tears to your eyes,
Turn your stomach inside out,
Make you feel so small, barely human,
That you'll wish you never even existed;
And that your only dream is to run away,

ZEK

To the ends of the earth,
In hopes where you could get away from constant nightmares,
Rest your mind, heal your heart, invigorate your soul,
And put back together the broken pieces of yourself
From the shameful sin that you have committed.
And so!
You take this shameful act and relive it
Every day for the rest of your days
In a confined small space.
And every time you try to forget your evil deed,
So you could forgive yourself
And free yourself from constant turmoil in your heart,
There is always someone there
Who creeps up behind you to remind you
Of your sinful act.
Your soul will never rest,
And not from all the pain and suffering
That you have seen and felt,
But from the wounds that just won't heal.
In hopes of alleviating the pain,
You tell yourself that God knows best!
That there must be a good reason
For your confinement in this dark place.
You seek to find relief and even peace,
Some explanation to justify this chaos in your life,
But deep down inside your wounded heart
It makes no sense,
What good can come from you rotting away
Alive behind these prison walls,
In such an unnatural way;
But you continue to persist and deceive yourself
By saying that God knows best!
And that all of these sufferings
Must be for the best!
But then it dawns on you
Like the first appearance of light in the sky

That you will never have a chance to live your life
To the fullest like every man should have.
The prison walls will always stand
Between you and your goals
For as long as there is breath in you.
The mental bondage of the chains
By which you are confined
Forces you to believe that you are a failure, a mistake,
A disgrace, not nearly human,
That you are a cancer tossed away,
That you are a slave for life
Who doesn't deserve to live a full, happy life.
And when you hear these words day after day
You start to believe subconsciously
That they are true,
And no matter what you say or do,
You have no voice,
You can't be heard or seen,
Even though you hear yourself loud and clear.
Every day feels like a loss
Regardless what you manage to accomplish.
It feels like part of your soul had given up
And left your body.
Time slips through your fingers like running water,
Lost forever!
And at the end of each day
You stand alone and all you feel
Is the cold wind with every bone
In your drained body.
You lay down to rest at the first sign of dusk
On the hard surface of the prison bed
With a heavy heart at hand,
And your head is filled with unsolvable dilemmas.
If you never lived behind the prison walls
Nor dug deep into the essence of your soul,
Then you'll never understand how it feels:

ZEK

To be confined in a cell as small
As the size of the bathroom for unknown time
Only knowing in your heart
That this is where you could one day die;
To be abandoned, forgotten in the hole for months,
Or even years like some kind of leper,
In complete isolation where men
Lose themselves out of desperation;
To be behind the prison walls
Is like being in a coma in a vegetative state,
Waiting and at times praying for someone to come
And pull the plug;
To relive the same nightmares over and over again
Without being given a chance to correct
Your life's mistakes,
And that no matter how many times you say you're sorry,
You'll never be forgiven
Until your sentence is complete;
And even then, you're abandoned, ostracized,
By the society for the remainder of your "free" life;
To build your strength out of what you can find,
But in the end, it leaves your spirit broken.
You start to realize,
But it's too late,
That in this beautiful life there is no place for you,
And that your life has been squandered by the pain
And suffering of your own making;
To see your loved ones pass away
Without a chance to say goodbye,
Nor attend their funeral,
Or to provide some kind of comfort
To the rest of your grieving family
Who are in desperate need of your help;
But all you can do instead is to stand
And watch helplessly from an endless distance;
To look and search for a way to find the strength

Within yourself so you can let go
Of your loved ones whom you failed to help
Because you love them so much that you dare not
See them suffer any longer
By staying and sharing your pain with them;
To start to look at yourself not as a man
Who helps his family, but as a leech,
Some sort of parasite who sucks and drains the energy
From his own loving family;
To go to sleep every night with unfulfilled dreams,
Knowing that when you wake up
You'll wake up only to the same soul-draining life,
Day – after – day – after day,
Until you just won't wake up one day;
To give up on your dreams because you know
In your heart that they will never become a reality,
Your dreams will always remain just dreams,
And never a reality:
And at the end of each day
It fractures your soul even deeper.
It robs you of your manhood, your humanity.
It makes you feel worthless.
It's a psychological castration.
Life behind the prison walls
Is a living torment, an eternal damnation
That dwells within the core of a prisoner's soul
That in the end, only death can rest his soul.
If you managed to dig deep into the essence of your soul
And didn't find the single darkest,
Most shameful secret in your life,
Then this much I say to you:
You simply haven't lived your life.
Not to the fullest as you might think.
For it's only the damaged one,
The one whose soul is gasping to stay alive
Every single moment

ZEK

From being ravaged by the life
That can truly comprehend what a man
Behind the prison walls is feeling
Deep inside the heart of his soul.

DAY II
THE CLOUD

I woke up to a ray of light beaming in my eyes and felt the warmth of it on my face. The full moon was long gone, and a bright red sun took its place. The first thing that popped into my head as I began to rise was my *díadía* Yúra's last words from last night before we said to each other *spákoinai nóchi!* (goodnight!). I was still confused to an extent by what he meant to say. Nevertheless, I was determined to make sense of it throughout my long day.

The breakfast was simple but rich and colorful with milk, tea, coffee, juice made out of different fruits, homemade bread, goat cheese and plenty of honey, and an abundance of fresh fruits from a garden that I planned to visit hopefully soon. All was set on the long table where I ate a slice of homemade bread with goat cheese and drank a cup of coffee with some milk together with the monks and practitioners as we all sat and shared our breakfast quietly. It was the best breakfast that I had with so many people, since the last time when I ate with this many people was back *v tyur'mé* (in prison) where I had to chew and swallow my food as quickly as I could before *mentí* (the guards) would start to bark demeaningly at me, telling me to hurry up before they kick me out.

After breakfast we headed down to the *zendo* to start the morning meditation session. It was a little different from last night, perhaps because I ended up sitting in the center of the hall instead of in the back, and I learned my lesson from last night to leave my pride behind as I took a posture of half lotus. I closed my eyes and began to meditate by taking in deep breaths. I filled my lungs with cool, fresh air that blew at me through the open windows on all sides. The people gathered calmly all around me as they took their seats, but I remained focused and undisturbed until the monks began to chant. I opened my eyes, and it was motionless all around me. The monks recited some kind of a short, rhythmic melody, a chant. I've never heard of it before. It went along these lines: "*Om mani padme hum…*"

It is said by the monks that those who find themselves in the deepest hell recite the mantra, "*Om mani padme hum,*" which refers to "the Absolute that is contained in everything." The *Bodhisattva Avalokitesvara*, who is one of the three pure sages and exhibits the virtue of compassion, dives into the deepest fire of hell to rescue beings from suffering.

This beautiful, harmonious, melodic mantra was what I needed to hear. It calmed me down and I felt even more relaxed as my mind stopped racing with distracting thoughts as it always does. *roshi*'s voice suddenly emerged and the euphonious melody began to gradually fade away.

"Do not get caught up in the fantasies, things that are not real. Recognize them for what they are, and as you do, let them go. Stop worrying yourself about problems that might never come. Stop assuming, speculating, driving yourself insane. When problems arise then you deal with them. But until then, stay in the present moment, stay awake and calm. Think of nonthinking! How do you think of nonthinking? By not examining. Not asking. Simply letting go and just resting your mind."

I became overwhelmed with deeper thoughts and unconsciously did the complete opposite of what he had said--trying to make sense of everything that had been going on *v mayéyi zhízni* (in my life). I was definitely doing, not nonthinking, but thinking over in my head instead.

My mind drifted and I visualized myself being in my own house, sitting on the porch in a Fat Boy chair, and drinking a cold beer with a redhead and a brunette, and before I could realize that I don't live in a house, nor do I have a Fat Boy chair, nor since when did I drink beer or ever chilled with these two broads.... I heard a loud crack, "Whaaaaack!!!"

Instantly, I felt a shock wave traveling throughout the back of my spine from the top of my head to my tail bone; every blade of hair on my body rose like I had been electrocuted, and if I had hair on my head, they too would've risen, and I would've looked like Blanka from the Street Fighter game.

Now I was fully awake, like I had just jumped into a freezing lake. My eyes were as wide open as the windows in the room, all thanks to the resonating cracking sound from the *jukpi* made by *roshi*. I could've sworn I saw a smirk on his face when he saw practitioners jump up. *Stáriyi chyórt!* (Old bastard!).

"Let go of whatever it is you are holding on to. Find the strength within you and come back to the present moment, to your breath, to this room, to the sound of my voice, to the smell of sweet, aromatic incense burning in the room, to the sound of the birds chirping outside these open windows. Listen to the leaves of the trees rustling from the breeze, feel a gentle wind on your skin. Wake up! Wake up! Wake up to this life."

Out of nowhere appeared a hazy cloud wafting over the *roshi*'s head. Or perhaps it has always been there, I just neglected to notice it. The cloud gradually grew larger from the three burning incense candles that were inserted in the pot in front of the Buddha statue. These three incense candles represent the *Triple Jewel*: the *Buddha*, the enlightened one; the *dharma*, the teachings of the *Buddha*; and the *sangha*, the community of the *dharma* followers, the monks, the nuns, and the practitioners, such as myself.

The smoke from the burning incense candles was floating up into the atmosphere like it was exuding smoke from a power plant and getting trapped up in the ceiling, creating a large, hazy cloud expanding in all directions like the cloud in the sky grows larger when it merges with other clouds.

ZEK

I stared into the hazy cloud and became mesmerized as it began to perform some sort of a ritual dance. It gracefully twisted and turned, glided from side to side as though some invisible celestial being transported itself from another realm into this one so it could mischievously amuse itself by taking control of the cloud with its supernatural powers.

I took a deep breath in and inhaled the sweet aromatic smoke of the cloud. The same hazy cloud that I was admiring so much was now in my head performing its ceremonial dance, and in the process, it started polluting my mind with thoughts of regrets from the past that I so adamantly try to overcome every day. In my impure mind, I found myself reliving over and over again the moments of my failures and mistakes. Imagining myself correcting the same mistake that caused me to end up *v tyur'mé* (in prison) for so many years. The mistakes that ruined not only my life, but also the life of my *mátushki* (mother). The mistakes that took the best years of both our lives.

I tried to resist the power of the cloud in my mind but failed. Somehow, I felt a strong, irresistible attachment to my past and continued to recreate it, fantasizing about it in many different ways where the outcome of my tragic *zhízni* (life) would turn into a happier ending. If only that mistake was never made. If only I had the power to sacrifice a part of myself, perhaps a piece of my soul, in exchange for changing the past so that the future would be different, brighter, and not as gloomy. I know it wasn't real. I even felt it in the heart of my soul. Nevertheless, I persisted indulging in the fantasies of my clouded mind until I heard a distant voice from far, far away calling me to come back, like I was lost in another realm. I recognized its warm, kind voice, and my heart began to feel the joy, for there was someone who cared about me after all.

"Let the past go! Don't dwell on it, it is a poison to your heart. What happened, happened. It is in the past, and you can't change it nor bring it back for any price. All of the mistakes that you've made, regrets you feel, harms you have caused someone else as others have caused harm to you—let it go! Or you will live in pain until you decide to wake up. By reliving the past and fantasizing about the future, you will miss out on this beautiful life that can only be experienced right here and now."

I felt his presence in my heart and mind. It was like *roshi* and the cloud were both in my head fighting each other for my life. The cloud was trying to seduce me with the gifts of pleasant dreams and taking me away from my wretched life by offering me a new beginning and a better *zhízn* (life), while *roshi* was fighting back for me to make me realize that only I possessed the power, the will, to change my desolate life and come out from the darkness into light.

He whacked the *jukpi* on his palm. The booming sound was so powerful this time that not only did the cloud clear from above *roshi*'s head but vanished into thin air right in front of my brown eyes, and I could see the Buddha statue looking back at me with a smile on its face.

The whole *sangha* had followed a tall monk into the garden where we began our walking meditation. We walked together, following each other's footsteps like a chain gang.

Behind the blackberry bushes I saw my *diadía* Yúra gathering the berries into a basket. I nonchalantly broke away from the *sangha* and went to see a friendly face.

"How is your meditation practice going?" he said and picked a few berries from the bush, handed me a few, and tossed the rest into his mouth.

"Full of fantasies and regrets," I responded disappointedly as I chewed.

"It will take time to improve, so keep trying." He paused for a second or two, looked straight into my eyes, and then up into the sky where the vast clouds were hovering over us blocking the sun, and said:

"When the cloud enters into a person's mind,
Fantasies arise and it becomes difficult to distinguish
What is real and what is not.
When the mind awakens,
It knows that it was trapped in a realm of fantasies,
And yet, it still returns to it again and again
With a desire to escape from the present.
When the realm of fantasies satisfies all of the mind's desires
It becomes easier to confuse and trick the mind,
And the longer the cloud remains to float in the mind
The darker it grows and harder it becomes
To let go and leave the realm of fantasies behind.
When the mind returns into the present realm

ZEK

From the realm of fantasies
And sees the realm of fantasies more appealing
Than the present,
It becomes frustrated, angry, and disenchanted.
When the mind overindulges itself on the fantasies,
Over time it becomes addicted to the escapism
And it is no longer the cloud
That dwells in the mind
But, instead, the brewing storm.
And when the cloud has brewed into the storm,
It begins to poison the heart and weaken the soul
And fill the mind with anxiety and gloom.
Life is no longer appreciated
And looked upon as a gift
But, instead, as a burden and a suffering."

Day II
Love

The *sangha* came back around the garden yard, and I resumed my walking meditation with them while *díadía* Yúra returned to his work picking berries from the bushes.

My left foot gently descended upon the ground as I inhaled a short breath followed by an exhalation after several steps as my other foot took a step. I felt the ground and every pebble under the thin sandals that I wore; and kept my eyes gently open, looking down consciously on the ground before I stepped forward with my feet so I, just like others in front of me, wouldn't step and accidentally kill any sentient beings that crawled on the surface of the ground.

We walked around the garden that was filled with many gorgeous trees. The scarlet red maple tree couldn't possibly be missed when the sun's rays stroke its leaves and majestically radiated its red, bright colors. The sugar maple and American red bud were also in my sight, and any living soul who passed them by couldn't possibly resist the temptation to pause and inhale the beauty that displayed in front of one's very eyes. These breathtaking goddesses that majestically paraded the colors of its leaflets has the power to restore any fractured soul and make any man fall in love with life again.

I stopped and stood alone, embracing for a moment with my eyes the pleasing colors of the trees' leaves, as calmness and peace rose within me, an elated feeling that I hadn't felt since I was a kid living with my *mátushka* (mother) in the northern part of Russia.

My *diadía* (uncle) walked up behind me with a full basket of berries and saw that I was somewhere else. Although I didn't see him at first, I felt his presence.

"*Ti znáyesh*! (You know!)" I said without turning around. "When you left *Rasíyu* (Russia) to go to the U.S.A. we were left alone. And although we didn't have much as I was growing up living alone with my *mátushka* in a small cabin, at least we had each other and that was enough for us to be happy at that time. Until she met a younger man, half her age, who then became her boyfriend; and then, my happiness suddenly came to a halt. At first, he appeared to be a good man. You know, a father figure. But then, when his charms wore off, he began to show his true colors. I was the first one to discover his evil nature that he so adamantly tried to conceal around my *mátushka*.

"An evil man cannot pretend for too long to be good amongst the kind people," *diadía* said, and placed the basket of berries on the ground.

"*Da*! (Yes!), I told her that he was no good. That he was not the man who she thought he was, but she only laughed and joked about me having an Oedipus complex. I wasn't mad, but I was heartbroken by her sarcastic words. I felt betrayed since I always thought that we had each other, but I was wrong. I understood that she was in love, and that love polluted her mind and made her blind from seeing her only son who loved her dearly; but instead, she cared more about that *kazlyé* (good for nothing/loser) than she ever did about me."

"Don't be too hard on your *mátushka*! *Lyubóv'* (Love) is one of the most powerful emotions that a human being possesses. It is extremely addictive, since once a person becomes under its influence, he or she becomes blind to everything else in life," he said.

"That wasn't the only thing she failed to see," I said, "since I saw in him what she couldn't see, not even when he put her in a hospital for a whole week; and even then she still refused to do a single thing to get rid of him from both our lives. I still can't grasp 'til this day, why in the God's name did she continue to stay with this kind of man? You cannot tell me that it was because of love! Since when one person is in love with another, he would not maliciously cause harm to another, and if he has, then that is no true *lyubóv*! That person's perception of love is perverted; and that is what my *mátushka* couldn't understand."

"It was like she was under a magic spell since every time when he abused her, she would forgive him and take him back. Although she would always swear to me, '*Bólshye nikagdá*! (No more!), I will not take him back this time, I swear to you, *móyí sin*! (my son!)'"

"The first time when I had my ribs cracked was when he kicked me as I was down on the floor after being dragged by the foot from one room to another from trying to defend my dear *mátushka* (mother).

"That day I remember as I was slapped around for talking back to him, I looked directly into his empty eyes, with the tears in my eyes, and with every loathe I had instilled within my heart and said to him, 'One day I will grow up, *súka* (bitch), and when I do I will punish you for every evil deed that you had done to me and my *mátushka*.' He froze for a few seconds for he didn't expect such deep words to come out from the kid's own mouth, and I could see the fear in his eyes, that I had put there, arising. Perhaps when I said those words to him, he had a revelation of some kind since neither I nor my *mátushka* were abused for the whole entire week since that day. And to be frank, I'm still proud of that day since that day was the first day in *mayéyi zhízni* (my life) where I had instilled fear in another man's eyes," I said.

"An evil nature in a man, especially in the one who hadn't worked on himself to eradicate his ill ways, cannot possibly be changed in an instant. It is a tremendous amount of work that lasts a lifetime," *diadia* responded and continued.

"Your *mátushka* gambled everything on *lyubóv'*, but what she failed to see was that any love that is based on the attraction of a physical beauty is not true love. For when the beauty starts to fade away, so will the love."

> "LOVE is like these beautiful trees,
> For by the time the autumn ends
> It will strip the colorful leaflets
> From the trees;
> And the beauty will disappear
> Like it never even existed;
> But if you fall in LOVE
> With the bare-naked trees
> When no one even looks at them
> Know that this LOVE
> Will last a lifetime."

"Your *mátushka* did the best she could with the way she saw life through her eyes. I tried to help from abroad as much as I could, but she was not easy to talk to, as you know yourself. It was always her way or the highway.

"I was very happy when both of you eventually arrived to America, but after you got arrested and were sent *v tyur'mú* (to prison) I started to look for a way out; and when I finally had a chance to leave the work that I did behind, I took it. The whole time while you were in prison, I couldn't stop but think how I have wasted all of my life hurting people to keep myself and others happy at the expense of others' sufferings; and that was just no way to live for any human being.

"The reason that I became *manáham* (the monk) was because of you. It was you who opened my eyes and made me realize how insignificant my life was!

"For 20 years that you've been away for the crime that I pushed you to commit…when I sent you to steal for the people who never even cared about you, me, or anyone else but themselves. Who simply use others until they can't use them no more; and when they no longer could use them they wash their hands of them like they did with you.

"Your *mátushka* blamed me for getting you involved with the criminal life and being sent *v tyur'mú* and she was right since it was I who introduced you to this criminal life!

"She died with the hatred in her heart for me and great love for you, as she waited for your return 'til her last breath on her deathbed. Her dying wish was to make me swear to her that I would help you find the right path in life, but how could I do that when I was lost myself? What you are going through right now I went through years ago with a single thought in mind—to become a better person so I could one day help you in some way. The same path that led me to find peace and calm, I also want you to follow.

"All I can do is guide you, and all you have to do is to try. No one can force you to do anything since it is only you who has the power to choose who you want to be and how you want to live your life.

"*Ti znáyesh* (You know), there is a Russian saying that comes to mind." He paused for a long few seconds to gather his thoughts and said:

> "Search!
> While you still have time,
> Live!
> While you still have purpose,
> Dance!
> While you still have a soul,
> Love!
> While you still have a heart."

DAY II
SUFFERING

We slowly started to stroll through the garden, and I felt as this was a perfect opportunity to take the weight off my shoulders that I had carried with me, God knows for how long. There was no one else left in my life with whom I could share my darkest moments, not since my *mátushka* (mother) had passed away. Besides, not many can understand what I went through, not like my *diadía* (uncle) who spent 25 years in the Siberian prisons. All of his *bratvá* (comrades) had died while being in the coldest, harshest prisons in *Rasíyu* (Russia), and this was no accident since all *zéki* (prisoners) who were sent there were sent only with one purpose: to make sure that none of them will come back alive. It was a death sentence right from the start, but a few who did survive and returned home were never the same. It was like part of their *dush* (souls) were missing, traded off with the Devil for their safe passage home. I'd looked into my *diadía*'s eyes when he came home from his last prison bid, and there was no light in them. It took some time for him until I could see the life in his eyes once again. I couldn't understand at first what was happening to him back then, but now that I had in some way walked the same path that he once had, I unequivocally understand the reason for his dark days.

The prison didn't kill my *diadía*, instead it made him stronger, stronger than any man I ever knew. His survival instinct and intellectual growth was much superior to his rivals that many of them feared him when he was around them. They feared him because he had an ability to see right through their *huinyú* (crap) and that was dangerous since too many powerful criminals feared him for exposing them for who they were to the *bratvá* in the criminal underworld. This was one of the main reasons why he left *Rasíyu* for he knew that there was no future for him there, only prison or death.

My *diadía* always had my back since I could remember, no matter how complicated things would get between us. He never criticized me for my mistakes. I guess he knew how easy it was to make them and then end up paying for them. That was something that no one gets to escape. Although, he always told me when I was a kid, "A smart person learns from other people's mistakes, while a fool learns from his own." I suppose that in the end we both ended up being *glúpami* (fools). It appears that both of us became so sick with our lives that he had to become a monk and I in the monastery following his footsteps. Although, so far I like what this Buddhist practice did to him since his guidance has been most enlightening. This was exactly what I'd been craving for, I only wish that I would've met this new person that my *diadía* became years ago before my imprisonment. Then, maybe I wouldn't even have had to endure all of these unnecessary sufferings.

"*Ti znáyesh chto, diadía* (You know what, uncle)? I must say that all of my improvements *v zhízni* (in life) occurred while I was in prison out of anger at life and hatred for all of those who caused me harm. I pushed myself as hard as I could with only one intent in mind—to get my revenge, revenge was always on my mind. I worked out so I could get stronger and physically hurt those who hurt me in the past. I studied diligently many subjects to sharpen my mind so I could destroy with my words the reputation of anyone who opposed me. I surrounded myself with the worst *zékami* (convicts) so I could learn the way of my enemy and become *valkóm* (the wolf) rather than *baránom* (a sheep).

"Part of me felt proud of improving myself and becoming a strong-willed man; but the other part was ashamed, ashamed because I knew, even though I didn't want to acknowledge, that I was poisoning myself with evil thoughts as I would spend days and nights fantasizing on my revenge. My greatest fear became to never be betrayed or manipulated by anyone ever again. Consequently, I began to feel on a daily basis greed, anger, and delusions attaching themselves to me; and I was becoming aware that I was rising to the same level of evil that I despised in other people since when I would look in a mirror, I would see in my eyes the eyes of the same persons who brought so much pain and suffering upon my life."

As I said this, I looked at my *díadía*. He was listening attentively, nodding his head, and then said to me:

"When we allow for an anger to arise, we become vulnerable to evil thoughts, and we become the first to suffer from it.

"Greed, anger, and delusions destroy all accumulated virtue, like a forest fire burns down all the trees that took lifetimes to grow.

"To overcome such negative thoughts, we must develop compassion and understanding that those who caused us harm through their wicked actions have allowed themselves to be defeated by the greed, anger, and delusions. We should feel pity for these people for they have chosen the path that will lead them into greater suffering."

"I wish we would've spoken about this many years ago," I said to him, "because by the time I realized how easy it was for me to bury myself in a grave than to dig myself out, I began to feel as there was no way out of this suffering that I myself instilled in me. I don't even know, to tell the truth, what made me snap out of such crippled mentality and eventually seek a different way to live my life. I guess all of the ill will that I have accumulated became more visible as I began to cultivate my virtue little by little. I must admit, at first, I had no compassion for anyone whom I saw suffering. I even had lost compassion for my own *mátushka* who would drown herself in tears from seeing me in prison for all these years.

I wanted no part with love since love, to me, was *nastayáshiyi ád* (a true hell), for when love was not reciprocated it turned to *yad* (poison) and my heart to stone.

"All of my young years I saw with my eyes what love did to my *mátushka* and I didn't want that for me. I was scared to turn into her. To live my life in a crazy relationship and then be left heartbroken like her after that *kozyól* (loser/good for nothing) used and abused her and then left her for a younger woman. Although I felt bad for her, the truth was that it needed to happen in order for her to wake up to reality. I'm glad it happened! I only wish that it would've happened sooner before I myself gave up on love and became overwhelmed with anger.

"*Ti znáyesh* (You know), for a very long time I couldn't understand the reason for my uncontrollable anger that I carried with me, but as I spent more years *v tyur'mé* (in prison), it dawned on me that it was from being poisoned by all of the physical and psychological abuse that I had endured and seen since I was a young kid. This was the real cause of my anger that grew and turned into hatred. My hatred became so strong that at times I couldn't even look at my own *mátushka*, although I loved her very much, but at the same time hated her for putting me *chérez ád* (through hell) at such a young age. Because of that experience, I turned my back on true *lyubóv'* (love) so many times that I became numb to this poisonous, and at the same time, amazing intoxicant. All that *lyubóv'* did was disturb whatever peacefulness was left in my mind and created illusions that further led to deeper suffering and delusions. *Lyubóv'* in my eyes was the cause for my true suffering…."

"And yet! It is the necessary suffering to further develop an awakened mind," he interrupted and added, "It is because of life's sufferings that you were able to strengthen your will since without suffering it destroys the will. For me, it allowed me to turn my misfortunate life's circumstances into the way of learning, understanding that I was only a human being and not a machine as at times we all tend to forget; and that I make mistakes and will continue to make them for as long as I live. But as long as I can learn from them and not repeat the same mistakes that cause me great suffering and even try to change them into positive by accepting them as an experience of a lifetime, I will continue to develop virtue and compassion until it will manifest into a greater awakening; and once you achieve the awakening, your soul will no longer be able to stand the presence of the wicked; and your mind will resist all of the temptations to fall back into ignorance.

"Our purpose *v zhízne* (in life) is to cultivate our *Buddha-nature* (the inherent potential in all beings to become a *Buddha*, the enlightened being) to achieve *moksha* (liberation from the cycle of reincarnation of suffering) and not to descend to the bottom of the ocean where suffering lies.

"I believe that the sole reason that you were able to recognize your ill ways and turn what you could around was that along with the evil seeds that had been planted in you by those who caused you harm, so were the good ones by those who loved you, since when the seeds began to sprout you were able to cultivate more of the good ones and continue to improve your life. Till this day they are growing and will continue to grow as long as you will nurture them, just like when you plant seeds into the earth and every day pour water over them."

We parted. He, I believe, headed to the kitchen with a basket full of blackberries that I'm looking forward to having for tomorrow's breakfast, and I back to my room to get ready for supper; but before we said *paká* (bye) to each other, he left me with these last words:

> "Suffering is part of life.
> Life is filled with worry, pain, and hopelessness,
> Causing suffering to arise
> Out of unfulfilled desires.
> Desires, the greater they are
> The greater the suffering.
> Eliminate the desires
> And the suffering will subside,
> Although will never entirely disappear.
> Suffering begins with birth,
> Increases with aging, sickness, and
> Ends with death,
> But then again begins with rebirth."

On the way to my housing, far ahead and behind dozens of scarlet trees, I saw a shadow of a dog and heard its cry like he was calling out to me.

Day II
Beast On a Chain

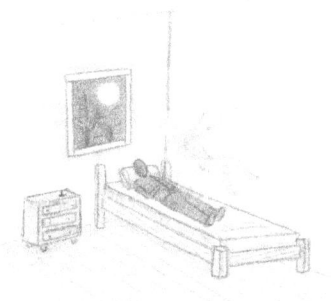

That night I desperately tried to fall asleep but couldn't even if my life depended on it. The barking of a mysterious dog that I heard earlier that day pursued to call on me even after dusk. I laid awake and patiently waited for the barking to cease but then decided to get up and go and see for myself the beast who kept me up throughout the nightfall.

I felt my spirit detach itself from my body as I rose from bed and floated out of my room. I passed through a long hallway and came out of the dwelling place and then entered the garden under the dome of a billion stars and hypnotizing red-orange moon. I walked through the garden of flowers and under the shadows of the trees as the moon's light helped illuminate my path. I wasn't sure to what direction I should go, but the barking cry guided me to find my way to him. And so, I walked until I saw the murky shadow of the dog and then he appeared out of the shadows of the trees, standing erect on all his four paws and staring straight at me with his piercing, water, human eyes.

He didn't move nor yelp a sound, instead he waited silently for me to come nearer; and when I did, his eyes began to glow like a fire and his razor-sharp teeth appeared scolding them at me. The dog was like a wild beast trapped in the place where he was, unable to break free from a rusty chain that went around his neck as the other end was nailed to the old, rotten tree. Part of me was glad that the beast was chained to a tree for it held him back when I began to speak to him; and when he couldn't get to me, he barked at me belligerently.

"Woof! Woof! Woof!" like it was I who chained him to a tree. And so, I said to him, as I boldly looked into his glowing, fiery eyes:

> Why do you bark so much?
> You drive everyone crazy day and night,
> Don't you know that!
> Do you bark because you're lonely, cold, hungry,
> Or is it because you're trapped against your will?
> I think it's all of that!
> But mostly it's because you're envious
> Of that black cat who sleeps on the same tree
> That you're chained to, and that it is free
> Like a bird whenever it wants to be.
> This same black cat that you chase every time
> When you manage to slip out of this old, rusted chain
> From time to time, and not because it is a cat,
> Or because you hate it out of your nature,
> But because deep down in your little dog soul
> You wish you were this cat;
> The same black cat that comes and goes as it pleases
> And enjoys its freedom day and night.
> The cat has no loyalty, no honor, no master,
> Or decency of any sort,

ZEK

It does the best to serve oneself and no one else;
And yet it lives freer than any decent man on earth.
The cat was born free just like you and I,
But here you are in chains like it is part of you.
And when this rusted chain slips off your neck,
The first thing that you do,
You go and chase the cat at lightning speed
To bite its tail off and seek revenge
For something that it had never done to you.
But your master! Your oppressor! The true Beast!
Who put you on this chain,
Who took away your freedom at young age,
Who ripped you away from your mother's bosom,
As you were still suckling milk
And stole your mother's motherhood for good,
Who put your father down of old age
Behind those old birch trees,
And till this day, since you were born,
Continues to subjugate, oppress, and show no regard
For your loyalty, obedience, respect,
That you had given him all your shackled life
Like your father and mother both have done
Long before you came;
And yet! You lick his hands from ignorance
And lower your eyes out of shame
When your mother, your oppressor, the real Beast
Appears in front of you,
And begins to condescend like he is God,
And you are his Dog for life.
You take your anger, your frustration out on a cat,
Not because you hate this cat, but because you know
That the cat can't fight back.
You want to hurt an innocent, poor cat
More than the real Beast who keeps you on a chain
Where you remain every day and night.
But when you're left alone, you cry!

Because deep down in your little dog heart
You know you hate yourself more than a cat
For not fighting back.
Poor dog!
I understand what life you have,
I truly do know what you're going through.
You see!
I too was once chained like you.
The saddest part I say to you,
That I can relate more to you, dog,
Than to any free man I ever knew.
Look at the scars on my ankles
Left from the shackles;
Look at the scars on my wrists
Left from the handcuffs
That once cut deep into my skin and made me bleed.
You have your chain and I once had mine,
The only difference between you and I,
Is that I know who my oppressor is.
The real Beast who kept me on a chain at one time.
You're a slave to this damn chain,
And the chain was once a slave to me;
Without the chain you have no purpose,
And without me the chain had no reason to exist;
Without being shackled and handcuffed,
I would've never known what freedom is.
It would've never come to light for me that—
The freedom is not given,
It's earned through pain and suffering from life.
Poor dog!
You don't even know most of the time
That you're chained until the chain
Slips off your neck, and then
You start to feel like you're not yourself;
You begin to miss this old wretched life
From not having it around your neck.

ZEK

You want this old, rusted chain,
That you have dreamed for so long
To free yourself from, back around your neck,
Since when you have it off
You don't even know what to do without it.
Without this chain, you can't dream of being free.
You feel connected to the chain like it's your home,
Your peace of mind that brings you comfort,
Calmness to your desolate life.
You feel more free in chains
Than you ever did without it,
But when you stopped fighting back for the dreams
That make you feel alive,
You let the rusted chain around your neck
Become a part of you, and you a part of it.
In your dog dreams, you dream of being this black cat
Where you climb trees, chase mice, drink warm milk,
And are treated with dignity and love by your old master,
As you place your head on his lap and then fall asleep.
You dream of small victories.
You want what others have.
No more. No less.
Perhaps the free life that you dreamed of
So many nights was never meant to come true for you;
But don't feel bad and don't you dare to give up,
As bad as things are for you,
At least you still have that old bone
At night to chew, and dream of life
That you could've had if only you kept fighting back.
Be grateful to this old, rusted chain
Strapped tight around your neck
That won't let you breathe at night with ease.
For it serves its purpose well to make you realize
How beautiful life around you is.
The saddest part I say to you:
I would've never known what freedom is,

ARTEM VASKANYAN

Unless I ended up like you,
Living a desolate, lonely life
Where only dreams would set me free at night.

Day III
Life and Death

I woke up in bed, soaked wet from sweat as the sounds of the gong rang in my head. I couldn't recall at all how I returned from the forest beyond the garden yard where I met the Beast on a chain chained to an old, rotten tree.

I headed to the breakfast hall and ate the pancakes with the blackberry jam and had a cup of coffee with a splash of milk. It went straight to my head, and I felt energized. After the silent breakfast I quickly walked to the garden to see if *díadía* (uncle) was back at work before the practice would begin. There were several monks in the garden, but none of them were my *díadía*. I walked further beyond the garden's red scarlet trees to see the place where I met the dog. Strangely, I couldn't find any sign of them both. I stayed for a little while walking in silence around the garden, and as I was passing by the grapevines, I looked and saw a green dragonfly trapped in the spider web, desperately fighting for his *zhízn* (life).

A true life and death experience displayed in front of my very eyes as the dragonfly vigorously beat his wings to free himself; but every time when he came closer to freeing a part of his wing from the web, a black spider the size of a silver dollar and with a white cross on her back would terrifyingly emerge from beneath the vines' leaves and suddenly attack by adding more of her sticky web to secure her prey tight in its place. The dragonfly fought back till his last breath as the spider mummified him with her silky web.

That morning I sat silently in the *zendo* and couldn't help myself but to think of that poor dragonfly who so desperately fought for his *zhízn*. In a way I felt a sense of guilt and shame for not helping him to escape his tragic fate. I guess when I saw that poor dragonfly trying to survive, I saw myself. When I was sent *v tyur'mú* (to prison) at a young age with no one there to watch my back and teach me how to survive; as I was left to my doom by everyone whom I knew, I fought with all my soul to stay alive. Yet, the only difference between the dragonfly and I is that I have survived while the dragonfly who fought so desperately to stay alive had lost his final battle.

Roshi's voice unconsciously emerged, interrupting my ruminating thoughts, and I reluctantly forced myself to let them go since I felt that a great revelation was unfolding itself in front of my eyes. Nevertheless, I returned to my practice.

"Nothing in life is permanent! Not your body nor your thoughts. As depressing and unpleasant as it may sound, ignoring the truth will not make your life easier. It will only hold you back even further and make your life more unpleasant.

"It is only through meditation practice that you become mindful and start to notice that death is only a breath away and that you are powerless against it.

"Once you become aware, you start to notice how precious the life truly is; and you will begin to appreciate and enjoy every little moment of this beautiful life even more.

"This awareness that you will develop over time will lesson your attachments to materialism, as you will realize that it is only a temporary gratification; and that in the long run it will leave you empty, as it will pollute your mind and cause you to suffer even when you do possess the desired object.

"Awareness will give you strength to let go of your attachments to the materialistic world; but most importantly it will help you face the death with a peaceful mind and grow closer to life with every breath even though the death has always been inevitably approaching."

Good words, I thought to myself as I tried to remember where I left my own thoughts so I could ruminate on them a little further.

"Don't forget that the whole point of meditation is to let go of your arising thoughts. Otherwise, you're not meditating, but fantasizing instead.

"The attachments that we have are not only to the materialism, but also to thinking."

On the way back to my room I felt bored to death from meditation. It all was still so new to me. The sitting for hours and staying mindful throughout the day was starting to take a toll on my mind and body.

I stood outside the dwelling place and was staring into the sky and watching the clouds floating towards the sun. I listened to a sound of leaves rustling from the late morning's cool breeze, crickets' shrill chirping sounds, and a woodpecker drilling with his strong bill at the tree trunk. A gentle wind brushed up against my robe and I inhaled fresh, cool, unpolluted air into my lungs and kept it trapped in my diaphragm; and as I held it in, I felt dispirited as it dawned on me that death was indeed only a breath away, and that it always comes when least expected.

Death suddenly knocked on my *mátushki* (mother's) door when I was still trapped in a prison cell. Last time when we spoke I took my time with her for granted, never telling her how I truly felt about her. Instead of telling her that I loved her, that I forgave her, that when I come back home, I will take good care of her, and that I will always be there for her, I was bringing up the past, the moments that put us at a distance, that crippled both of our lives. She tried to apologize. She tried to say *prasháyi* (goodbye) as if she knew that Death was outside her door waiting impatiently for her. But I didn't let her speak, for all I wanted was revenge. Someone to blame for the mess that I had brought upon myself by my own actions. Nothing good came from my harsh words, for every wicked word that I had thrown in her face backfired in my face 10 times the fold, and till this day when I start to recall every last word that I said to her, I begin to choke and feel the dagger in my heart twisting.

> My heart shattered like a porcelain plate
> Dropped to the floor,
> Blood froze in my veins like a lake freezes over
> From the cold winter,
> Lungs became breathless like a cave
> Without an exit,
> Stomach churned like an evergreen tree
> Shaken by the angry wind,
> Eyes became lifeless like a desert
> Without a drop of rain,
> Lips trembled like an earthquake
> Convulses the land,
> Soul darkened like the storm clouds
> Fill the bright-blue sky,
> When I received a letter from my uncle
> Stating that my *mátushka* had passed away.

I held my breath in like it was my last, not wanting to let go, to get closer towards the end. Not just yet! There are still so many dreams to achieve, oceans to cross, lands to roam, people to meet, life to live, before I end up like that dragonfly trapped in a spider web whose *zhízn* (life) has been gradually drained out of him. And as I held on to my breath with every spirit that I had left in me, it occurred to me that even this breath does not belong to me. It is like I'm borrowing it just to stay alive a little longer so I could fulfill my yet undiscovered purpose; and if this breath does belong to me, then why do I have to part from it?

I held on to my breath until I began to feel faint. I slowly exhaled and quickly gasped for another breath of fresh air and felt rejuvenated. I guess life goes much smoother after all when you don't hold on to things for too long. *Zhízn* (Life) is just like a breath, you have to let go to start living again.

ZEK

On the way to my room, I saw my *diadia* in a hallway. He was standing on the ladder and cleaning the windows from the pollen that the wind blew inside the house from the garden. The white rag that he was cleaning the windows with was covered with yellow dust, and as he dipped it into the bucket of no-longer-clear water, the water turned even yellower.

I snuck up behind him to surprise him, to say "*privét!*" (hi!), but when I tapped his foot with the tip of my fingers, he jumped! The ladder moved sideways, and I saw his eyeballs popped out and his mouth opened wide as he made a sound that sounded like when you try to break a board with a karate chop and miserably fail.

"Oi! Oi! Oi! Oi!" he yelped.

I instantly grabbed the ladder and stopped it from moving sideways, as it was about to fall with him on it.

He gave me the look! You know, the look you get from your *mátushka* when you do something bad.

"*Ti menía chut' ne pribíl!*" (You almost took me out!) he said, placing the hand on his chest and exhaling with a heavy sigh like he just dodged a bullet.

"*Izvení!* (Sorry!) All I wanted to do was to surprise you."

"Oh, you surprised me, by giving me a surprise heart attack!"

"Yeah, but if you would've died, you would've been reincarnated."

"*Da!* (Yes!), but then I would've started the whole process of finding my path all over again."

We looked at each other and broke out laughing.

"Oh, *pizdétz!* (Shit!) am I glad that you didn't fall. I don't know who was more scared, you on the ladder or me on my feet."

"Scared! Oh, I wasn't scared! I had everything under control. As a matter of fact, I saw you sneaking up behind me."

"Yeah right! So that part where your eyeballs were dropping out of your skull was all part of your stunt."

"*Nu da!* (That's right!), and I don't understand why you were scared. It was me who was on the ladder and not you!"

"*Da!* But can you imagine what would've happened if you would've fell and broke your old hip. I would've got blamed for it. The news would've read: 'An *ex-zek* (ex-convict) broke an old monk's hip.'"

We both laughed, and as he was wiping the tears off his eyes with his fingers and I was wiping mine, I saw that happiness is a choice just like a long-time suffering.

"*Oi! Pizdétz!* (Oh! Shit!), I haven't laughed this hard since the last time I saw you before I got locked up," I said.

"Anyway, I was hoping to bump into you, and I don't mean literally; but I wanted to ask...."

I told him about the dog on a chain that looked like a beast who kept me up all night with its loud barking; and whom I went to see farther behind those red scarlet trees. He glanced at me with a perplexed look and said, "My dear nephew! We have no dogs nor any dog who might look like a beast, especially on a chain. I don't know what you had seen, but it must've been some kind of eerie dream."

Confused I felt, and as I thought it over in my head; perhaps he's right! It must've been a lucid dream that felt so real that it etched into my memory till this very day. "Never mind," I said and changed the subject once again.

"So, I was wondering if you could expand a little more on life and death."

"That is what I'm here for," he said smiling, and climbed down the ladder.

"A subject on life and death is not easy to grasp for any man for as long as he clings on to life with everything he has. It requires for a person to let go of his old ways when he feels that he is not on a right path; and have the courage to try a different path, just like you've done when you realized that the path that you were on was not doing you any good."

He paused to gather his thoughts and before he began to speak again, I looked into his green eyes and saw a different man. It wasn't my uncle's spirit that I saw in them, the same spirit that laughed and joked with me minutes ago, but the other one, the one that always comes to life when he begins to ruminate on life.

Death is only a breath away
That's what the Buddhist monks like to say;
But when you do become aware
That death is on its way;
Do you start to wonder

ZEK

How and when you're going to die?
Do you panic?
Lose sleep and appetite?
Perhaps you stress all day
And even try to run away?
Cursing that damn day
When you became aware
That death was only a short breath away;
Or do you choose life
And begin to celebrate your awakening
By embracing death with a smile;
And start living and enjoying
The rest of your life while it lasts
With each breath as it's your last.
If you do choose life
Then you'll see!
That where is death
There is life to be,
And where is life
There is death to see.

Day III
Pure Mind

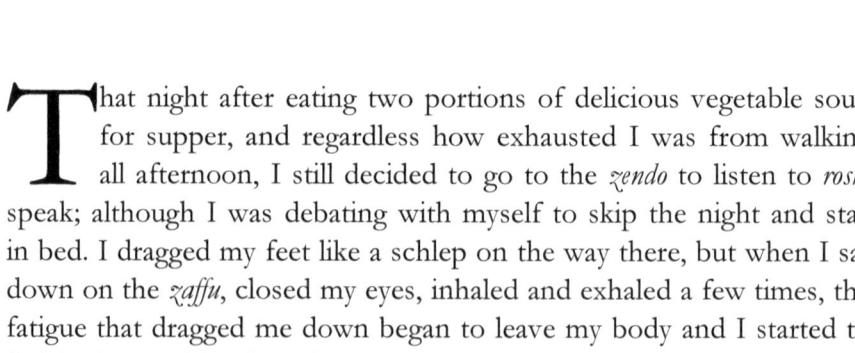

That night after eating two portions of delicious vegetable soup for supper, and regardless how exhausted I was from walking all afternoon, I still decided to go to the *zendo* to listen to *roshi* speak; although I was debating with myself to skip the night and stay in bed. I dragged my feet like a schlep on the way there, but when I sat down on the *zafu*, closed my eyes, inhaled and exhaled a few times, the fatigue that dragged me down began to leave my body and I started to feel invigorated by the spirit in me. As I sat motionless, the chatter and the commotion from people around me gradually dissipated, and the only voice that I began to hear was of *roshi's*.

"So, how do you become enlightened?" he asked, looking around the room for someone to respond, but instead heard nothing but coughs and sniffs and crickets. Realizing that is all he is going to get for an answer, he continued.

"In order for you to attain *Nirvana*, reincarnation in the pure land of a total extinction of desire and suffering; first, you must become enlightened, become one of pure mind, a mind totally free of greed, anger, and delusion.

"This can be achieved through the power of silent meditation practice by reciting the *Buddha's* name '*Amitabha*' (Infinite Light) where during this practice you can reach the point of *samadhi* (pure concentration), a state of which the mind is free from all distractions as it fully becomes absorbed in itself.

"When you recite the mantra, you become united with your mind, body, and spirit as you uphold *Amitabha* in your heart.

"Not only does this meditation practice tame your mind, but it also sows virtue, wisdom, and dissolves accumulated evil *karma*.

"In addition, you must also accumulate good *karma*, actions that lead to your reward in the future. *Karma* includes a thought, a word, and a deed that in its time comes into fruition just as you plant a seed that grows into a tree and then begins to produce fruits.

"Everything that happened to us, or will happen, has been already set in motion by us through our *karma* that we have caused directly or indirectly in our past.

> "If you want to know
> Your karma in the past,
> Then look at your present;
> And if you want to know
> What the future's consequences will be like,
> Then look at your karma
> In the present

"In order to cultivate your mind so it would become purer, you must live by and apply on a daily basis the five general rules in how to properly behave. These *Five Precepts* are: Not killing; Not stealing; Not misusing the senses; Not lying; and Not misusing intoxicants."

"Can you elaborate on the Five Precepts?" a young lady with braided hair, sitting in the front row, asked with a trembling voice.

"Certainly! And thank you for asking," *roshi* responded excitedly as he adjusted the sleeves of his robe.

"The first precept is not killing. This rule might appear easy to follow, however, if we are to apply this practice to all sentient beings, then it can be quite a challenge. Think of the insects that we crush under our feet when we walk. Flies that we kill when they land on our food. Mosquitos that bite us at night, which I myself killed a few last night."

While everyone chuckled and giggled, I was looking into the sky through an open window, and as the smell of rain wafted in the air it made me think how I've spent years amongst murderers, people who have broken this sacred precept of not killing, and what I had discovered about them during my imprisonment was that most of them committed this horrible crime for their own personal reasons. Some killed out of hatred, some out of envy, and some even out of love that turned to poison when they realized that they had been betrayed, deceived by the one they loved. Some killed deliberately, and some accidentally, just like when any one of us steps accidentally on the insect and kills it.

I came to realize that those who have committed such horrible crimes, whether it was done deliberately or not, were no different from any other criminal who was there with me for much less serious crimes, since every and each one of us, whether *v tyur'mé* (in prison) or not, has the potential to take a life. I believe that the reason why some didn't was simply because of their ability to remain mindfully aware of their actions, which gives them an upper hand to think of their consequences before they act; or that they simply haven't found themselves in dangerous situations where they would've committed such a cruel act.

"The second precept: do not take that which is not yours. In other words, don't steal. Stealing is motivated by the desire to have something that you don't have. It is a craving that causes the mind to deceive, be dishonest, and disrespect those who have a desired object that you have your eyes on. It causes you to become greedy, and the best way to fight such temptation is to give away some of your possessions to those who are in need. In time, such practice will cultivate generosity, honesty, and lessen attachments to materialism."

When *roshi* spoke about the second precept, I couldn't help myself but to think of my past. The past that I don't talk much about but always find myself going back to—a life of being *vor* (a thief).

There is a saying in Russian, "*vor v zakóne*," (a thief in law). In other words, a criminal who does what he does because that is all he knows how to do; or you can also interpret it as a criminal who lives by the code of thieves.

I turned to that lifestyle since I was a young kid because that was all I saw around me. Everyone that I knew was *vor v zakóne*. My family, friends, my mother's boyfriend. I didn't even realize how many people around me were *vorí v zakóne* (thieves in law), or even who I was until I got caught and arrested many years later when I was an adult living in the U.S. I thought that I lived a normal lifestyle since that is how all of my family and friends lived, with only one rule—don't get caught! But if you do, then keep your mouth shut since the life of a thief must not only be kept unknown to the outsiders, but it is also sacred.

At first, I stole because I needed to survive, it became my livelihood. But then I started stealing out of greed, and not because that's who I was, *vor* (a thief). Eventually it manifested itself into something else. It became much more than just stealing for me. It became a way to find my peace of mind, and I became addicted to stealing.

"The third precept," *roshi* continued, "is: not misusing the senses. Not overindulging yourself with food, beautiful scenes, smells, sounds, and sex.

"The sexual behavior in particular is one of the strongest cravings out of all senses, for it has the pleasure of all the five senses, form, sound, aroma, taste, and touch.

"It is considered to be a burden to our mind, for it interrupts its peacefulness and prevents us from attaining a pure mind."

When I was locked up, there were a lot of moments when I thought of nothing else but *zhénshin* (women) and the promiscuous life that I would have once I was released out of the prison. Just a thought of it would disturb my mind, send me into a state of depression, and at times it would enrage me, for I felt like I was being psychologically castrated by the prison system that kept me on a chain like a castrated *sabáka* (dog). And when I was finally out and free, *shlyúhi* (whores) were always in my bed, which made my life only for a brief moment satisfied, but in the long run I was back to feeling empty and depressed again.

Come to think of it, I guess I was and still am afraid to have a long-term relationship, since in my mind I already have established that it won't last. Why waste both of our time and in the process get hurt? I chose *shluh* (whores) then and now because it is a brief relationship without any commitment, and the best part of it is that when I wake up, I feel free and never guilty like I'm deceiving another woman.

"The fourth precept is: not lying, abstaining from the words that are hurtful and untrue; words that include shouting, insulting, sarcasm, and slander. But instead cultivating words that help to develop friendship and peace, encourage people to do positive deeds.

"By being mindfully aware of the words we choose to say, we can abstain from the speech that we might regret later in our *zhízni* (life).

>"Buddha said,
>'If you know anything that is hurtful and untrue,
>Don't say it.
>If you know anything that is helpful and untrue,
>Don't say it.
>If you know anything that is hurtful and true,
>Don't say it.
>If you know anything that is helpful and true,
>Find the right time.'"

Throughout my life, whether I was living with my *mátushka* (mother) or being *v tyur'mé* (in prison), shouting was all I heard. Constant arguments, gossip, and frivolous conversations that by the end of the day just hearing such slanderous conversations made me feel agitated and empty; and even though I stayed as much as I could from such chatter, I did find myself reluctantly being affected by it. I remember when I said harsh words to my *mátushka* that I didn't even mean to say but did it anyway because at that time I was hurting and wanted her to feel my pain as well, feel what I felt once when she hurt me by her actions. In a way I was getting my revenge without even realizing that by doing that I was digging two graves, one for her and the other for me since both of us in the end were hurting and my harsh words that I said to her that day didn't make me feel any better, but only worse. Till this day I'm ashamed by the way I behaved. I guess that was the result of the karma's effect on her. She reaped what she sowed, and I reaped what I sowed. This karma cycle just never stops!

"The fifth precept is: not misusing intoxicants, abstaining from alcohol and drugs because they weaken our ability to remain mindfully aware of the things we say and do, which then leads to bad decisions and causes us to suffer.

"The most dangerous out of all five precepts is misusing intoxicants since once a person is under the influence of drugs and alcohol his mind becomes unconscious and easily deceived; and it is at this vulnerable moment when a person can lie, misuse the senses, steal, and even kill."

This was so true, I thought to myself. I clearly remember when I used to say and do things that were so hurtful and untrue when I was under the influence of drugs and alcohol, that if I wasn't under the influence of them, I would've never even dared to think in such an ignorant way. As a matter of fact, it was usually after using *narkatú* (drugs) or drinking *bukhló* (booze) or both at the same time that made me become numb to the arising thoughts that tried to talk me out of my wrongdoings. Although intoxicants did help me to avoid dealing with some of my inner pain, it was not as much as when I was breaking the second precept. Stealing was my fa*vor*ed drug. When I would get high off my drug, I would then completely forget the dagger that was lodged in my heart. I needed my drug, my adrenaline rush, to pump through my veins so I could be in control, feel alive and free from my internal pain, and in the process orchestrate my devious plan to steal from whoever's name I would find on my list to be robbed that day.

My *narkatá*! (drug!). It would give me a sense of belonging in this world, since I desperately wanted to matter and let people know without actually telling them that I existed. When I was under the influence of my fa*vor*ed drug, emotionally I felt very powerful, like I was the only person in this world who could see the man I'm about to rob. The same man who thought that he had everything under control like he was an omnipotent being who considered himself to be better than any *chelavék* (man); but only to realize in an instant that it was all a big lie invented by him just to make himself feel a little bit better about himself; and I was that person, that unknown *chelavék* who possessed that power to change his destiny and transform his *zhízn* (life) from being a self-confident man who felt like he was on top of the world to a little, fragile boy who was now at the bottom of it desperately crying on the inside from losing the only thing that made him feel like he was a shining star amongst the fallen. That thing was always different for everyone. For some, it was their mama's jewelry, or their *bábushka*'s antique painting, or a dirty secret written in their diary hidden under their pillow, and for many others it was always their *déngyi* (money) that was either hidden in the shoebox under the bed or in the closet. But whatever it was that made them feel like they were omnipotent, I would always find it and take it from them and replace it with a feeling of emptiness. An emptiness that only I would know about before they would even discover it for themselves. All I had to do was to destroy a man's confidence and that was enough to make him weak and fall apart. To have this ability, this gift, to take what is precious to someone, was like having a taste of king's power while sitting on a golden throne.

The truth is that it never crossed my mind to think about the victim's pain who would wake up or come home only to discover that their *déngyi* or precious jewelry or cars were long gone. I would have my *díadia* (uncle) sell the stolen items to his connections and have stolen cars disassembled at Misha's Chop Shop during the night and sold for parts or shipped out of the country in the ship container back to *Rasíyu* (Russia) while I would be laughing my ass off as I would be getting drunk on Smirnoff and high on *anashé* (marijuana) with my *bratvá* (brotherhood) and spend my hard-earned *déngyi* at the strip club on *shluh* (whores).

At times when I would be chilling with my *bratvá* in a club, I would meet some of the people that I robbed and hear them whine while faking a sad face and acting with empathy, and at the same time laughing on the inside and think to myself, *durák*! (idiot!). What kind of a *bandít* (thug) leaves his safe unlocked or writes in his diary that he had cheated on his wife with two *shlúhami* (whores), or one of my favorites, hides *déngyi* in a shoebox under the bed? Yes, of course, no one expects to get robbed, but when you're involved in a criminal life, you must always prepare for the worst and never forget that it is all a matter of time until you will get robbed by someone like me, or worse, arrested by *mentámi* (the cops).

The truth is that many *vori v zakóne* (thieves in law) get too comfortable at times, and above all, too cocky, thinking that they are untouchable like they have a license to commit crimes without consequences. Even I, although I always took my work seriously and never bragged to anyone about what I did or how much money I made, eventually got busted when my best friend dimed me out to *mentám* (the cops).

I guess the true reason why I never felt bad about my victims was because they weren't as innocent as they portrayed themselves to be. They were either *vori v zakóne*, vicious gamblers who looked for a way to avoid paying their debts, or simply made a business deal but never delivered on it. The bottom line was that they all owed, whether it was to my *diadía* or to *pahán* (the boss). In either case, someone had to collect the debt and I usually was the guy for the job, since I was very discrete about our operation and only dealt with my *diadía*. But then I started to get too cocky and rob criminals who did not owe simply because I could and because when criminals get robbed, they don't call *mentám*. At times, they don't even tell anyone because of pride and not to show weakness amongst other *varóv* (thieves) that they were robbed.

My *diadia* blames himself till this day for me going *v tyur'mú* (to prison), but you cannot get someone in trouble whose every fiber of his body is craving to feel alive as he is willing to do whatever he must to break away from the chains that were suffocating him; and what set me free was being that *vor* (thief). Although, I must admit that this profession was vile in its own way, but it was a necessary evil to keep me sane in my own way. *Da* (yes), I did it out of ignorance and selfish reasons to help myself to keep my brewing storm content. I blame no one for what happened to me, since no one pushed me nor made me choose that path. I did it because part of me enjoyed it.

I guess I did it because I wanted to be free from the pain and suffering that was consuming me. For once in my life, I was in control. That I finally had a purpose and that I mattered in this selfish world, although the internal pain that I wanted to get rid of so bad did not leave for any price. Instead, it grew thirstier and hungrier with every job I did. It wasn't long after that until I found myself trapped, addicted to the escapism of robbing without ever seeing a way out of it, until one day when I was *v tyur'mé* (in prison), I realized the pain that I inflicted upon so many people by my wicked actions when I myself was robbed. Something very precious to me was stolen. And it wasn't *déngyi* (money) nor *narkotá* (drugs), but my wallet with the only photograph of my passed-away *mátushka*. When I discovered that her photograph was stolen from me it was like reliving that horrible moment when I found out that she was gone. It dawned on me that instant that I will never see her lovely face again. I must say that it tore my heart and pinched my soul that day. That till this day I feel it in my heart and soul. However, it was because of this soul-depriving moment that I became aware of the wrongs that I had committed, and I swore to never steal again.

Roshi interrupted my thoughts….

"The lesson here is that we will all at some point or another break our vows, but for as long as we can recognize our wrongs and be mindfully aware of our actions then we are still on the path of developing our pure mind.…"

…Like I was saying! I understood the value of one's property when I fell victim to the robbery myself. When my wallet with the address book was stolen which contained the information of my family and friends, and the most valuable part was a photograph of my *mátushka* and me that we took together the time when I was still free.

I wasn't mad at the thief who stole from me as I should've been. Instead, I quietly sat down on my bunk and said to myself, I deserve what has happened to me! Now I know how being robbed feels. For I have caused to so many this same pain that I would feel lame if I were to complain.

Karma is *súka*! (a bitch!), but a necessary *súka*. In my case it made me realize the poison that I've been to so many people. Ever since that day I've been grateful to the thief for opening my eyes, since once my eyes became open, I never stopped to become better. I never went back to my old ways. I despise that old life that I lived, although I'm grateful to my past, for if it wasn't as bleak and lonely, then I would've never experienced such brief enlightenment of seeing my wrongs. I would've always been stuck in this perpetual cycle of ignorance.

ZEK

DAY III
UNDERSTANDING

As we returned to our meditation there were many thoughts that I couldn't escape from. One in particular that kept storming my mind and that I tried to let go but found too enjoyable to indulge in, was when I was *v tyur'mé* (in prison). As I was there, what stood out for me the most was how the multitude of *zékav* (convicts) although brave, lacked the spirit to fight for their *svabódu* (freedom). It was as if when they gave up the fight they gave up on their lives and forgot where they were and who they were; and when that happened, they became *rabámi* (slaves) to their own never-ending misery.

When inner pain has been suppressed and treated with self-destructive antidotes such as taking intoxicants, gambling, lying, stealing, and engaging in frivolous conversations, and by any other means to numb the inner pain, then with time the pain increases and the war within oneself escalates. As I gradually managed to improve myself and move on from self-destructive ways, I began to look down at those who sought to escape. I judged and criticized many *zékav* in my mind, not considering the fact that they all struggled with their inner pain and looked for a way out of their sufferings as I did. They used the only tools that were available to them to solve their manifesting problems. But as I reflected on my own *zhízn* (life), I realized that I wasn't that much different from them. Not too long ago I was a proud *vor* (thief), although I was never much for a drinker or a drug user or even a gambler, since I always threw up after drinking too much, got too paranoid from using drugs, and always lost when gambling. However, I did get my high off stealing. Stealing was my drug. It was my way of neglecting to deal with my inner pain, just like many other *zéki* (convicts) did in their own way.

I was a hypocrite for judging others to deal with their problems in their own way. Just because it wasn't my way, I looked at them from a cynical point of view. When I judged others without fully grasping the pain and suffering that they had endured throughout their lives, I was acting ignorant just like the prosecutor, the judge, and the jury. The same *troika* (trio) who charged, convicted, sentenced, and sent me *v tyur'mú* (to prison) without grasping the true reasons for my wicked actions.

> They could not see the reason
> Behind my wicked actions,
> For they did not know
> What I went through in my life;
> For if they did,
> Then they would have understood
> The reason for my wicked actions;
> And would not judge me
> So harshly as they did.

It was only during my time *v tyur'mé* did I truly begin to understand why people were driven to use intoxicants and do what they can to seek an escape from reality. I always tried to keep an open mind by asking myself, what drives *chelavék*a (a man) to turn to *narkatyé* (drugs) and to *bukhlú* (booze)? Most think that addiction to intoxicants begins with smoking *sigarétii, anashú,* (cigarettes, marijuana) or drinking *píva* (beer) that in time increases an addiction and makes a person turn to use stronger intoxicants. This may be so, but what is the reason that drives a person to turn to such intoxicants in the first place? That is what I was grappling within myself to figure out.

I figured why search for answers elsewhere when everything that I needed to know already lay within me? Why look for a patient and a doctor when I have them both already present in me? For me, my addiction to stealing was caused by internal pain that built up over prolonged years of physical and psychological abuse, as well as neglect. Addiction to stealing was a way to numb my pain and help me to take my mind elsewhere, just like it does for *narkamánu* (a junkie) and *alkagóliku* (a drunk).

V tyur'mé (in prison) every single *zek* was addicted to something. If it wasn't to *narkatyé* and/or to *bukhlú*, then it was to food, religion, exercise, gambling, or like in my case, to poetry and education. Eventually I became a *vor*acious reader and a poet writer who, just like everyone else, was trying to escape the life that I didn't want to live. But at least my addiction was doing some good to me. It expanded my mind and made me view the world from a different angle where ignorance for me was no longer bliss, since I understood what was causing me to suffer, only I didn't know how to put a stop to it. I felt blessed for making progress and applying education to *mayéyi zhízni* (my life), but the more I learned the more I felt incomplete internally from not being able to do more with *mayéyi zhízni*, since as my wisdom increased so did my sorrow.

The self-education that I have found for myself helped me to pay closer attention to my surroundings and not engage myself with the prison politics, where a bunch of *zéki* (prisoners) were gossiping amongst themselves like old women about other *zékav* (prisoners).

Through excessive writing, I found myself tapping into my inner-self and brought some of my long-forgotten suppressed memories to the surface, since writing poetry helped me to understand myself better as a person. It said, "You cannot move forward without letting go of your past." But how could I do that when all of my answers to understand myself lie in my bleak past?! Digging cold-heartedly into my past through writing and being true to myself with my actions was what made me realize who I once was, nothing more than just an angry and confused young man who was pissed off at the world and all the people who lived in it, particularly with those who traumatized him and caused him to grow bitter.

V tyur'mé (The prison) administration always tried to make *zékav* (convicts) feel ashamed of themselves, particularly when they showed anger, telling them that being angry is wrong! That it is a horrible sin that must be abolished! I always disagreed with this crazy ideology because if a man *v tyur'mé* is not angry from being deprived of his basic human needs, like having access to medical care, education, work, healthy food, spending time with his family, and being kept *v tyur'mé* with draconian sentences since a young age, then there must be something horribly wrong with that *zek* who is not showing any sign of anger. It is the same as to accept his miserable fate and give up on fighting for his *svabódu* (freedom). Any *zek*, any man who is treated inhumanly has a right to feel anger, frustration, and feel sick from being screwed by the prison system from every direction. The truth is that everyone in prison is angry. The only difference between *zékami* (prisoners) who are angry and those who are not is that some were able to find a way to suppress their emotions through positive actions, while others did it through negative actions.

The saddest part from being incarcerated was seeing how young men were gradually destroyed by the prison system by sending them deliberately to the maximum-security prisons where they were forgotten. For many young men this caused them to ultimately fall further into a dark path just because they had committed a violent crime or simply were being marked by the *mentámi* (cops) as gang members, or as in my case with *Rúskayi kriminál'nayi organizáziyi* (the Russian organized crime), while *nasílschiki* (rapists), *pedofíli* (pedophiles), woman beaters, drug dealers, and especially *krísyi* (rats) all went to minimum-security prisons where they had access to education, better food, medical care, and everything else that the maximum prisons didn't have.

Being marked as a part of *Rúskayi kriminál'nayi organizáziyi* without any proof, only that I was *Rúskyi* (Russian) and that my *díadia* (uncle) was investigated on suspicions of being one, made me end up being marked as one and consequently being sent to maximum-security prisons where I was completely lost for many years. I felt what every *zek* felt who was trapped in their cells. Desperate, alone, confused, and angry; suffocating at night from the trauma that once was caused upon us, by the trauma that we caused upon others, and from the constant stress that was manifesting itself into the trauma that we would all have to deal with in the future. And for me, that future is now, and I'm dealing with it, along with the nightmares that are still lingering and the pain that still persists without any sign of subsiding. It is sad how many young men who entered into prison were left to rot there by the "justice" system. The same system that magically expects them to transform themselves into some kind of angels before their release day from a soul-wrecking place that did nothing but oppress them, and where many young men ended up spending all of their young years being there fighting to survive to see another day. It was sad to see how many *zékav* (convicts) became wicked, turned into someone who they never were in the first place, simply because the "justice" system neglected to fully understand them.

I must admit that I enjoy ruminating on my errant thoughts, since at times I feel uncomfortable to share what I truly feel with other people. Even with my *díadia* I won't discuss my most profound moments of *mayéyi zhízni* (my life). Not that I don't trust him, but because I feel too ashamed to share what lies in the heart of my soul with any man.

The most profound moments of *mayéyi zhízni* that I had experienced was in a tiny prison cell where it all came with a price of deepening my sorrow even greater. The self-realization gradually took its toll on me after I relentlessly continued to dig deeper and deeper into the core of my *dushí* (soul), and in the process reopening the wounds that had been long forgotten. I know it sounds melodramatic, but after many sleepless nights I felt as if my life was slipping through my fingers like water, and no matter what I did, I felt jaded. I was just like any other *zek* (prisoner) with a dark past who was trapped in a cage to deal with his internal problems. However, the only part that was different about me was that I, along with a handful of prisoners, understood a bit clearer that what I do here and now will affect me for the rest of *mayéyi zhízni*; and to that I owe it to my honesty. I don't even know, to tell the truth, where all of that courage came from that gave me strength to look at myself directly in the mirror and admit my wrongs.

I can proudly say that all of those years that I've spent *v tyur'mé* (in prison) were not a complete waste of time, for when the night would engulf the sky and the silence consume the living, I would begin to ruminate on my life and understand myself even further. Although, at times, I would wish that I would've remained in a blissful ignorance, not understanding *zhízn* (life) nor myself at all, since once my insight grew, an unimaginable feeling of agony would arise like there was a dagger lodged in my heart; and I would fall into a place of total despair; and within this hopelessness, I would find my way to bring myself into lightheartedness, and being true to myself was the key to reach what I call my brief moments of enlightenment.

Just like the seeds of good amongst the bad ones that were planted in my mind by those who were close to me and over time grew from bad to wicked and from good to virtue; so did I, having done exactly the same to those whom I was close to. When I was angry and hateful, I passed these negative energies upon others. I became no different than those wicked fools, those same ignorant persons who passed their evil energies upon me; and as I gained some insight, I realized how I had no right to loathe any man even if he is wicked, for I'm guilty of inflicting pain and suffering upon others just as it was done once upon me.

What became clear to me during my rumination was how forgiveness starts first with self-understanding, and the process of forgiving others cannot be fulfilled unless one forgives oneself.

Prior to ending up *v tyur'mé* (in prison), being a thief was the solution to all of my ongoing problems. It was my remedy, my cure to my never-ending anger and prolonged suffering from life's long traumas. The decisions that I made to choose a path of being *vor* (a thief) was the only path that I could see at that moment. Of course, there were other options, but I just could not see them at that time. It was like I was blind, although, I saw clearly what was in front of me, but only all the wrong things.

As I sat in the prison cell, I often ruminated as I do now in the meditation hall by comparing my lifestyle to the life of a young dog. I wondered back then, and I wonder now, what if you were to chain a young *sabáku* (dog) and place it in an isolated, dark, cold place, and in the process traumatize it every single moment up until it has matured into a fully grown *sabáku*; and then, let it off the chain to roam freely amongst the people. I guarantee you that it is all a matter of time until it will bite someone; and when it will, who is here to blame for such a wicked act? Is it the dog, or is it the owner who traumatized *sabáku* (the dog)?

If nowadays the society holds the owner of the dog responsible for its wicked actions, then why isn't the society holding the guardians of the young man who has committed wicked crimes responsible? Instead, they are thrown into the mercy of the "justice" system where the prosecutors, the jury, and the judges are ignoring to understand the reason of the young man's wicked actions; and since none of them have ever been in the young man's shoes, thus the result is that they often bury them in prisons with the draconian sentences thinking that this must be the only solution to the existing social problem.

It is because of the "justice" system's ignorance that young men are still being prosecuted to the full extent of the law instead of trying to understand the real reason for their criminal behaviors.

> In their eyes,
> A vile act must be punished
> With a vile sentence that they call justice.
> They try to drive out darkness with darkness,
> Without understanding that only
> Light can defeat darkness,
> Love can defeat hate,
> Peace can defeat violence;
> And that any man
> Can act like a violent dog,
> If he is treated as one;
> Just like any dog can act humanly,
> If it is treated as one.

ZEK

Day III
Virtuoso Vor (Thief)

That night I had lain in bed haunted by the ruminating thoughts that continued from earlier that night as I tried to meditate, but instead was engulfed by my errant thoughts.

There is a storm I feel inside of me, and it has been brewing for some time now. Too long to even remember when and how it had begun. From time to time, I tend to fall into a moment of feeling shame from allowing myself to fall into the hands of ignorance. The shame turns into disgust, and then an anger arises as it brews into a storm.

For a long time, I blamed others and even deliberately, just to take the blame off myself. I tried to run away from my existing problems by ignoring their existence as a whole in hopes that they would disappear in their entirety; but now it makes me laugh from the way I used to think, since to try to run away from my problems was like to run away from my own shadow. No wonder my problems never left me, but only continued to accumulate and grow larger like a cloud that just won't pour rain.

Ever since my mother's boyfriend came into both of our lives, I then discovered the true essence of anger living within me. After being tormented by this *chudakóm* (bozo) throughout my young years, I was left to deal with my brewing storm all on my own, never fully understanding the cause of my anger brewing within me, or how to control it, or how to move on from it. As I struggled to think clearly and think before I acted, at times my mind would become so frustrated because of it that I would begin to make irrational decisions, followed by the grave mistakes that till this day I feel disgusted with myself for making them. However, as difficult as it might be for some to believe that when I became *varóm* (a thief) my anger would subside and the brewing storm would disappear from my mind; and I would forget completely all of those who hurt me, and even at times forgive them. It was like I was transformed into a different person, free from anger and nightmares and polluted thoughts.

I've robbed, not because I needed to steal in order to survive financially, but because it was my only cure that I had discovered for myself to contain the brewing storm within me. As a result, I without realizing became addicted to stealing, since when I didn't steal, I would find myself waking up in the middle of the night angry at the world and with an insatiable desire to go out and rob some unlucky *vará v zakóne* (thief in law). Being *varóm* was my curse and my salvation. I miss it like the junkies miss their drugs. *Ya lyublyú* (I love) living on the edge, trying to find a way to control a situation that I never had control of in the first place. The feeling of the adrenaline rush pumping through my veins as every molecule in my body becomes intoxicated by what is yet to come. The unknown! It was the combination of several substances. The fear of unknown, the pleasure of anticipation, and the most important part, forgetting. Forgetting everything and everyone who I abhorred from causing my mind to dwell on pain and hurt; and instead, only remembering one part: how to meticulously execute the duty of the virtuoso *vor* (thief).

My skill required of me to be stealthy, unnoticed, and unheard. Many of *varí v zakóne* (thieves in law) believe that any one of them has a potential to become a virtuoso *vor*, but I believe that it is one quality that is not for just any man to possess. I would even stress that one must be born with it. To be a thief,

> You need sharp eyes.
> To be a good thief,
> You need sharp eyes and quick hands.
> To be a great thief,
> You need sharp eyes, quick hands, and brains.
> But to be a virtuoso thief,
> Not only do you need all of the above,
> But also a peaceful mind,
> So peaceful that you could hear
> Your own heartbeat.

Unfortunately, the latter part was never in me. No matter how much I tried to achieve it, I just couldn't get to that level. Perhaps I was too damaged right from the start. The disquietedness that I have always felt inside of me would never let me become the virtuoso *vor* that I so hard pushed myself to be.

It was *tyur'má* (the prison) that gave me some of the peacefulness that I so often craved. How ironic that turned out to be! One place that I never thought that I could benefit from gave me what I was looking for all along. But one thing about the prison is true is that it will destroy a man, or it will build him into a man that he only dreamed of becoming.

> And,
> Just like it is only inside the furnace,
> Under the extreme conditions of heat
> Can the soul of the katana be truly forged,
> And bind itself with the sword;
> So is the same for any man who seeks
> To fully develop one's soul,
> And bind it with his mind and body,
> Can only do so when his soul
> Dwells in the most extreme conditions
> That is unknown to men.

ZEK

To be a thief in prison was and is considered as the lowest of all crimes that *zéki* (convicts) could commit. However, it all depends from whom *zek* steals. Is it from another *zek*, or a prison guard? For as long as it is not from another *zek*, being *varóm v tyur'mé* (thief in prison) can be quite resourceful. When I got a job at the kitchen, I decided to put my skills to use. I took great pride at what I did, since the prison administration was always feeding 'us' *zékav* (convicts) very poorly, forcing employed *zékav* at the kitchen to serve on line small portions of food to other *zékam* (prisoners); and the food was always unhealthy and poorly prepared. Always overcooked vegetables, rotten fruits if we had any, chicken or beef stew without any meat in it, molded bread, and at times even curdled milk. Everything that was served on the kitchen line for *zékav* just sucked. And it was this bad food that made everything else *v tyur'mé* (in prison) even worse, while in the guards' kitchen their food was fresh, healthy, and delicious. The prison guards would cook the books and order this type of food on the prisoners' food budget; and of course, none of the prisoners would ever be served this type of food unless they steal it.

Every time when I would sneak in into the guards' storage room, I would steal what I could. I've stolen so much from that place that I could practically write a book about what and how I've stolen. Every other day I would manage to bring something to my block where I lived and share it with my fellow *zékami* (cons) who had none. I felt like I was a Robin Hood, stealing from the rich and giving it to the poor. First time *v mayéyi zhízni* (in my life) stealing felt right. It felt right in my heart, mind, and in my gut, especially when it was empty. But the best part of it was the look on the guards' faces when they would open their storage room and discover that they were robbed once again by the Robin Hood; and then watch them eat *tyurémskayu yedú* (the prison food) with the distorted faces, and that was priceless! However, the downside of stealing was that on the next day *tyurémskii mentí* (the prison guards) would retaliate. They would come into our blocks in great numbers, usually early in the morning while everyone was still asleep, to do a major shakedown. They would trash our *klétki* (cells) and in the process strip search us.

There hasn't been a single *zek* in the prison system who hasn't been strip searched by *tyurémskimi mentámi* (the prison guards) on multiple occasions. Strip search, by the way, is nothing more than a sexual assault, because when *zek* (a prisoner) is forced to perform a strip search, he must:

Remove all of his clothing to be checked for "illegal" substances; spread his buttocks (ass cheeks), followed by squatting and forcing himself to cough; lift his scrotum, show his penis as he's told to pull back the foreskin to show the glans of his penis; and if the guard is sadistic, he would demand for *zek* to put his fingers in his mouth and force it to open wider by stretching his (face) cheeks and stick his tongue out after touching his private parts.

Such forced exposure of himself in such an indecent, sexual way in front of another person(s) causes every *zek* to feel ashamed and suffer mentally afterwards. Till this day I feel ashamed to what had been done to me. Strip search is a sexual assault which is a crime, just like any crime that a man commits and ends up in prison for. Yet this crime happens every day within the prisons, and no one is ever held accountable for such disgusting crimes against another *chelavéka* (man). This makes me wonder if *zek* were ever even considered to be *chelavékam* (a man) while being in prison?

Day IV
The Crossing

After a good night's sleep, I woke up invigorated and hungry. I went to the dining hall and had a quick breakfast, followed by the meditation practice and then discussions about the Four Noble Truths. After the practice I decided that instead of going back to my room or to the garden for a walking meditation, I would rather go for a stroll under the cloudless azure sky and the bright shining sun. I walked farther to the east side of the garden that I still hadn't had a chance to explore, and as I continued to walk, I heard mellifluous sounds of a stream and followed its echo. It led me further away from the monastery until my eyes could no longer see the dwelling place where I stayed. When I saw the brook, I approached, and my eyes followed its shallow, swift, clear stream. My mind completely let go of the existence of time and what it's like to be in a constant rush.

The stream brought me to a dilapidated bridge that must've been a hundred years old. This ancient bridge rested on both sides of the two hillocks, and the brook that led me to the bridge now transformed into a river passing swiftly underneath it. It didn't look safe, since the bridge swayed from side to side from a light breeze; and as it swayed it made the squeaky sounds like it was about to fall apart. Nevertheless, regardless of how unsafe it looked and sounded to me, I, out of my inquisitive desperate desire, wanted to cross to the other side and see more in-depth the beautiful flowers that covered the top of the hillock; and the farther I gazed, the more impatient my spirit grew to go across the bridge.

I began to cross the bridge with extreme caution, moving like a turtle on the beach sand. I took one step at a time on the decrepit wooden platforms with a fear that I would fall through the rot. I gripped tightly with my hands to the thin railings made out of ropes and clenched my teeth; and each step that I took the platforms squeaked, the bridge swung, and the ropes sounded as if they were about to rip apart. The bridge appeared to be much shorter in length when I was not standing on it, and I felt as if I'd been crossing it for many hours, when in fact, it must've been only seconds at the most.

Why haven't I stayed back at the monastery like the rest of the practitioners and practice walking meditation with the monks? Why do I have to always get myself into some trouble? If I was to fall through the rotten wooden platforms, I wouldn't even be able to yell for help, since I'm miles away from the monastery. No one will ever hear my cry!

Great doubt was growing within me as I thought of myself as a failure. This wasn't the first time that I thought of myself in such a self-destructive way:

> Ever since I fell from the tree when I was young,
> I became bound to the fear of heights;
> And as I stood in the middle of the bridge
> That could collapse at any moment,
> I once again was overpowered by the fright.
> My hands shook, knees buckled, head spun,
> I became short of breath and

I profusely began to sweat.
A great doubt arose within me,
As it reminded me of that day
When I fell from the tree and
Became bound to the fear of heights;
Do I have what it takes to transcend
The part of me that fought within myself
As I was the enemy who stood in my own way
From crossing this dilapidated bridge?

It was my awareness that made me feel emotionally unpleasant from being in danger, and of course, the fear of heights. I worried about myself because I was concerned for my safety. It was my mindfulness which allowed me to experience the essence of myself, as self, the ego; and when my ego arose, so did the fear, since it was the fear that threatened my self-importance; and until the ego is defeated, the ego, as self, that causes the fear to arise, will continue to dominate.

I heard the ripping sound of the ropes coming apart and swiftly hopped across the bridge like a grasshopper; and as both my feet landed upon the soft green grass with flowers all around, instead of the shallow brook with sharp rocks, pure joy overwhelmed my fear, and I did a quick tap dance.

Day IV
Four Noble Truths

      Across the hillock and beautiful red-yellow flowers, I walked and came to a path that took me to the narrow alley between the pink flowers of the Hall's Hardy Almond trees that were no higher than my waist; and the Torn Triple Crown Blackberry bushes whose large, juicy, sweet berries I couldn't resist as I indulged myself on eating quite a handful of them; and as I stood and ate my lunch, I saw a hummingbird beating its wings at incredibly fast speed over an Angel Trumpet bush's flower and extracting the nectar (the same sweet liquid that bees gather to turn it into honey, and that once was called the elixir, the drink of gods by the Greeks) with its long slender bill from inside the yellow trumpet flower's glandlike organ.

      I heard and then I saw a colorful woodpecker drilling through the bark of an evergreen madrona tree as he or maybe she clung at the top with its massively strong claws to the bark, producing loud, chiseling, rapid sounds across the forest. Meantime, the madrona's leathery, glossy leaves rustled playfully from the warm breeze and reflected light from the rays of sunlight, displaying flashlight images to all directions, just like when you see a light entering a brilliant and traps it within its numerous facets.

The flock of sparrows flew over my head and simultaneously descended on the madrona tree's branches and began to feast on its orange-colored berries.

A cardinal, a finch with a crested head, short, thick bill, and bright red feathers, swiftly landed on the leaflet and stared directly at the small round meadow behind the bushes.

I followed the finch's gaze to the meadow and saw an old man and not a decaying tree as I at first thought to be. He was standing erect not on his feet, but on the crown of his head. I looked at him with much inquisitiveness as did the finch, especially when the old man started to transition into an inverted lotus posture as he slowly slipped in his other foot into a full lotus while remaining standing on the crown of his head, accomplishing this posture, a headstand with both legs crossed in a full lotus.

I was hypnotized by the old man's performance and felt like I was a fly being pulled by the bright light. I stood motionless, not to disturb the natural process of living creatures that Mother Nature manifested right before my eyes. I took such an awe-inspiring scene as a gift, an opportunity to learn and appreciate life through such a vivid, colorful experience.

I have seen the beauty of nature ever since I've lived in *Sibíri* (Siberia) in the northern part of Russia, but I have never appreciated such exquisite scenery displaying before me as I am now. Now, as I look around me, not only do I notice the essence of the nature with my own two eyes; but I also feel it with my heart, mind, and soul, as I feel my existence in being as I am. Before, it was like looking for the stars in the middle of the day, knowing in my heart that they are out there, but just not knowing when to look for them. I felt as if all of the senses in me had been awakened. Now, not only could I see, smell, taste, hear, and touch, but I also felt as if the power of the sixth sense arose within me, making me feel like I was outside the bounds of my physical senses.

I stared at the old man inquisitively when a sudden flashback reminded me the words of *roshi* that I heard earlier this morning at the *zendo*.

"The essential part of Buddhism is based on the *Four Noble Truths*. A practitioner must know them by heart in order to fully grasp the essence of the Buddhist practice.

"The first part of the Four Noble Truths is the existence of suffering. Meaning, we are born, get old, get sick, and eventually die. We need to realize that we are born sick and for as long as we are being reborn, we cannot escape the perpetual cycle of pain and suffering throughout our lives.

"The second part is the causes of suffering, which creates an illusion by making us believe that if we only possessed whatever it is that we desire, then our lives would become better, and we would be much happier. We need to ask ourselves a simple question: What is that desired thing, a craving that makes us ill; causes us to lose our grip on reality and suffer? We have to identify our disease, the desired 'craving' that causes us to suffer, so we can start treating ourselves.

"The third part is the cessation of the causes of suffering. It is the feeling that is caused from possessing the desired cravings from its uncontrollable attachments.

"We need to believe that we can bring to an end the suffering and get well, that there is a remedy to cure our sickness. This is realizing the truth about *Nirvana*. That a total extinction of desires, pain, and suffering are possible; and that there is a way out of the perpetual endless cycle of birth, death, and rebirth, the *samsara*.

"And lastly, the fourth part of the *Four Noble Truths* is the path that leads to the cessation of the causes of suffering. Living in a way that will help liberate us from being controlled by our cravings and bring into existence the causes that will help us to attain *Nirvana*.

"We need to find that medicine that will help us cure the disease and get us to the path of freedom."

I stood engulfed in my own thoughts, thinking over what *roshi* had said earlier this morning, until I was suddenly brought back to the present moment when the old man began to unlock both of his feet from the full lotus and gracefully transition himself by coming down from his pose to his feet. He did the entire movement with such elegance and ease that he made it look like any man could do it; and those who know that they could not would feel quite envious of him, like I did. I tried to stand on the crown of my head before but failed many times, for if it wasn't the balance that made me fall, it was my lack of concentration. All it took was one faulty thought to send me falling down to the floor.

From the distance I could see his long grey beard reaching down to his waist, swaying side to side as he started to walk toward me. His entire body struck a resemblance to a skeleton as his skinny arms and legs seemed like tree branches hanging from the decaying tree. He was short, a little taller than a blackberry bush, wearing up to his knees an underclothing of some sort.

"*Namaste!*" we both said and bowed to each other holding our palms together vertically in front of our chest. As we approached closer to each other, I saw a thin face with a scar across his eye. It was the color of the murky water, and his other eye was as green as the grass we were standing on. His eyes were evenly protruding out of his eye sockets from living an ascetic life. The ascetic practice includes: wearing shabby clothes; eating only begged food, and only one meal a day, along with living in a secluded, solitary place, under a tree, or in the open; and sitting only, never lying down. This was the price the ascetic has to pay to achieve his enlightenment. Through such extreme practice of self-denial and self-mortification according to the doctrine, it leads to a higher spiritual and moral state and releases the ascetic's soul from being bound to his body.

His eye shone with wisdom and simplicity from abstaining from luxuries and pleasures, and constantly overcoming the desired cravings of the restless mind. His face looked like it had seen better days, but it also looked modest, with moral standards and spiritually polished by the years of abstinence from the pleasures of life.

Being in the presence of a real ascetic, a person who dedicated his life to the practice, made me feel eager to know more about life and how to find a meaningful path. But somehow, I was getting this vibe as if there was a space of energy, an invisible magnetic field, between us that prevented me to approach closer and ask. Only a moment ago I was full of life, excitement, revelation, but now I feel as if my soul was stung with a venomous sting. I couldn't think of a single question. Not a single thought entered my mind. Where are my restless thoughts now? The overwhelming thoughts and questions that don't let me sleep at night. I couldn't utter nor yelp a sound. It was as if I had lost my tongue to speak; and then, there was a moment of lingering silence.

He must've noticed how much I've suffered within myself and gestured for us to take a seat on the soft blades of grass right where we both stood. A quiver of excitement, and at the same time an eerie feeling, stormed my mind when he began to speak.

Every word that he uttered came in syllables. It sounded like a drum. I felt the drumbeat in my head. My heart beat like it was the beating drum, and his rhythmic words flowed through my veins like a stream runs into the river. It was as if my soul got drunk on the Armenian wine from Yerevan and began to sing and dance as it lifted my spirit up, and I felt full of joy and life from the words that sounded like a beating drum.

He said, or more like chanted, to be exact:
"It-is-a-cy-cle-of-life
To-be-born-get-old-get-sick-and-die;
To-cling-to-the-de-sires
To-our-in-sa-tia-ble-cra-vings
That-in-the-pro-cess-cau-ses-us
To-break-the-mo-ral-five-pre-cepts:
To-kill,
To-steal,
To-mis-use-our-sen-ses,
To-lie,
And-mis-use-in-to-xi-cants;
We-tend-to-de-ceive-and-force-our-selves
In-be-lie-ving-that-if-we-at-tain-our-de-sires
Then-our-lives-will-be-filled-with-ha-ppi-ness,
It-will-cease-our-su-ffe-ring;
But-with-time-we-come-to-re-a-lize-that
It-only-sa-tis-fies-us-for-a-mo-ment
And-in-the-long-run-brings-us-even-grea-ter
Su-ffe-ring-and-pain-as-our-a-ttach-ments

To-the-de-sires-in-crease-with-each-day;
There-is-a-cure,
The-way-out-of-sam-sa-ra-in-to-Nir-va-na,
It-does-exist;
The-me-di-cine-that-cures-dis-ease,
It-lies-with-in-us,
We-all-po-ssess-the-po-wer-the-will
To-free-our-selves-from-the-cau-ses-of-su-ffe-ring;
We-must-be-lieve-that-we-will-find-the-cure
And-li-be-rate-our-selves-from-the-su-ffe-ring;
We-have-to-lead-a-life-style-that-will
Gra-du-a-lly-e-ra-di-cate-the-cra-vings;
Those-same-a-ttach-ments-to-the-de-sires
That-wea-kens-our-sen-ses-and-cau-ses-us
To-su-ffer-all-the-more;
The-way-to-end-the-su-ffe-ring-is-through
The-prac-tice-of-the-Noble-Eight-fold-Path."

The old man gently shut his eyes and so did I; and I began to meditate under the luring chanting sounds made by nature's creatures.

Day IV
Between Two Realms

A sudden bolt of energy rushed through my veins, and I was pulled into a space between two worlds, one of his and one of mine. My body and mind felt as if they belonged to someone else.

> For many years that I've been away,
> Living in between two realms,
> One of life and one of death
> And not pertaining to either or,
> Made me look at each—
> From a cynical way;
> Where instead of seeing the beauty
> That dwells within each soul,

ZEK

I only saw the ugliness, the evil that dwells within;
I couldn't help myself but to see all souls
Within both realms through the obscure lens;
And often wished to never live
In either one of them again;
But I was wrong to think
In such a self-destructive way
I see this clearly now;
For I never felt more alive
Than I did back then;
It was that unknown space
That lingering, ageless moments
Of existence and events—
Of past, present, and future;
And being in between the life and death
That made me appreciate the importance
Of two realms.
That fire and ice that burns and freezes
And agelessly lingers in each moment of time,
Is what makes me hold on
To my last breath,
To my last sanity,
To every pleasant moment from my past
As it brings me to my knees
To pray for a lovely dream
In hopes to escape a dreadful night,
Was when I truly found myself being alive;
That burning fire,
That freezing ice,
That unknown space between life and death,
Between the freedom and captivity,
Is life,
And it can only be found
While being in between two realms
And not in either or.

Not quite sure for how long I sat ruminating on my lingering thoughts, but when I gently opened my eyes to the mellifluous chants of the finch, the sun was no longer above my head, but setting in the east instead; and the old man was gone, only a decaying leafless tree stood not too far away from me in the middle of the lea.

Day IV
The Noble Eightfold Path

I headed west following against the current of a shallow mellifluous stream as I crossed the dilapidated bridge without a fear in my eyes. By the time I came back to the monastery, to the dwelling place where I stayed in, the nightfall was heavily approaching, and I felt tired on my feet.

I walked through the garden where monks and new practitioners were mindfully practicing the walking meditation. Part of me felt guilty from not being there with them and practice as I was supposed to as a group; but the other part of me felt proud, since I'd gained some insight into my life, and that in time I hope it might diminish my suffering, and possibly even lead me to the right path.

I entered my room, lit the candle, and sat on the corner of my bed and ruminated on the long, captivating day. I wondered,

> When a man is reborn into the realm
> Of pain and suffering,
> He is welcomed with joy and happy tears;
> But when his spirit departs from his body
> And leaves the realm of pain and suffering behind,
> He is parted by unimaginable grief
> And weeping tears;
> And that makes me wonder!
> For whom these grieving tears are spilled.

A loud knock on the door disrupted my train of thought.

"Come in!" I said with an exhausted voice.

The door opened and my *diadía* Yúra stepped inside the room.

"*Kak ti!* (How are you!) Are you ready for the meditation practice to end the night?" he said and closed the door behind him.

"*Ésli chésno tho net!* (To be honest, no!) My feet are killing me from walking all day long; and my mind is just burned out, it's overwhelmed with so much information that I just want to crawl under my sheets and stay in bed for the rest of the night," I said and leaned against the wall.

"*Slish!* (Listen!) No one ever said it will be easy, because easy doesn't get you far in life. It is only those who push themselves to the limit who get to benefit from their hard work in the end. It is good that you are searching and looking for answers and trying to find your path. You are doing exactly what the Buddhist practice requires of you.

"*No znáyesh chto!* (But you know what!) Keep one thing in mind, that it does not matter how hard you try to find your way in life. If your mind is not genuinely with your desire to change with all your heart, and to abandon your old ways that hold you back from living a happy life, then even if you think you are on the right path, you really are not; and in the end, it will lead you to nowhere and not where you really wanted to be.

"Put all of your energy in paying attention to your mind rather than your body. Your body is selfish, since it always puts itself before 'you.' Your body wants to make itself happy, while your mind wants 'you' to be happy, as it always thinks what is best for you.

"The bottom line, don't let your body be in control of your mind."

My *diadía* has a way to get people motivated in the same way as he did back then. It's like let's get going and get things done, or if not, then take a hike. But his motivating words worked on me just like they did back then. At least just enough for me to get up and move around the room.

The fatigue began to leave my tiring body. His encouraging words were exactly what I needed after all to get me back on my feet. We both left my room and headed to the *zendo* for the evening practice.

The illuminating light from the moon shone through the open windows as the evening sky swirled over us, putting my mind at ease. We both sat in the front row and began to meditate as *roshi* smacked the *jukpi* twice on his palm. His voice sounded sharp and loud, bringing me back to my awareness, as I listened attentively to him speak on *The Noble Eightfold Path*.

"*The Noble Eightfold Path* is the *Fourth Noble Truth*. The path that ultimately leads to the cessation of the causes of suffering. It teaches how to live in a way that will free us from our desires and how to find that essential medicine that will lead us to liberation from suffering.

"*The Noble Eightfold Path* consists of three groups, they are *Wisdom*, *Morality*, and *Meditation*. These three fundamental paths must be worked on simultaneously to develop the path to freedom.

"There are two parts to the *Wisdom*; the *Right View* and *Right Thought*, which cannot be achieved solely by listening to what other people say and by watching what they do, or by simply reading books. It involves a much deeper experience.

"To gain *Wisdom* first we must develop a *Right View*. Understand the importance of all life's existence in the world. That all living beings strive to escape suffering, and that it is our view of the world that forms our perception to choose our path, since it is we who are in control of our *karma*.

"The second part of the *Wisdom* is the *Right Thought*, which allows us to think in a positive way. By helping others, we subconsciously change ourselves from egocentric to altruistic. We can train our mind through meditation practices in order to replace negative thoughts with the positive; and through good karma eradicate negativity that is caused by the attachments and desires.

"The second group of *The Noble Eightfold Path* is *Morality*, which has four parts to its ethical conduct, *Right Speech*, *Right Action*, *Right Livelihood*, and *Right Effort*.

"*Morality* has to do with being honest with ourselves. See ourselves as the human beings who are gentle and not perfect; and that by repressing our negative emotions we will only fail to understand why our mistakes had severe consequences.

"One of the four parts of developing *Morality* has to do with *Right Speech*. Paying attention to what we say and being mindful of our negative arising thoughts. By abstaining from lying, frivolous conversations such as gossiping, sarcasm, and slanderous speech that hurts others, will generate within us positive attitude.

"To cultivate *Right Speech*, we must learn how to be patient, honest with ourselves, and most importantly, understand that it will take time to eradicate our old self-destructive habits that we had acquired throughout our lifetime.

"The second part of developing *Morality* has to do with *Right Action*. It is about behaving mindfully in ways that our actions won't affect the living beings in a negative way.

"To cultivate *Right Action*, we must not only practice to have positive thoughts, but also act in a positive way. Think mindfully before we act.

"The third part of developing *Morality* has to do with *Right Livelihood*. It is about acquiring our wealth in a legal, nonviolent, honest way that won't bring harm to other living beings.

"To cultivate *Right Livelihood*, we must think of others before we think about ourselves.

"The last part of developing *Morality* has to do with *Right Effort*. It is about applying ourselves just enough to reach perseverance. If we apply too much of our energy then we will grow weary and fail at our task; and if we don't apply ourselves enough, then not much will happen.

"Our energy must be distributed evenly in order for us to succeed at our goal. We must find the middle way by not trying too hard or too little. Otherwise, we will be struggling all of our lives and failing at our goal.

"The last, and the third group, of *The Noble Eightfold Path* is *Meditation*, a mental discipline that consists of *Right Concentration* and *Right Mindfulness*.

"*Right Concentration* allows us to focus on our mind without any distractions and see the world for what it truly is.

"*Right Concentration* is developed during meditation practices, preferably in a quiet place. Focusing on a single mantra, a place, or a subject that we picked to meditate on.

"While *Right Mindfulness* is being aware of our environment and of ourselves, we must find the strength within to disperse our negative thoughts that pollute our mind; and eliminate the delusions, as well as clear our mind of all thoughts that arise during meditation.

"We have to be disciplined to tap into a state of calm and concentration during our present moment. The process of staying conscious requires of us to feel our body, our breath, our heartbeat, our pain and pleasure as our emotions arise; and instead of trying to repress them or escape from them, we embrace them and become aware of them.

"By being mindful it allows us to understand what causes us to be happy and what gives rise to our suffering in our lives; and since everything starts with the mind, all thoughts that arise ultimately will lead us to actions. Bad thoughts, bad actions; good thoughts, good actions. Recognizing our thoughts and letting them go is being in a state of *Right Mindfulness*.

"*Meditation* allows us to discover our inner-self and become familiar with our mind. It tames our flustered mind to a point of total concentration, calm, and mindfulness.

"This internal process develops consciousness and understanding in what triggers our stormy emotions to arise.

"Essentially, the mental discipline is all we are ever going to need on our lonely journey."

By the time *roshi* was finished I was half asleep, pretending to be meditating. My *díadía* pulled my sleeve to wake me when he heard me snore. *Roshi* lost me somewhere around *Right Speech*. After this night I have even more respect for the monks who practice daily, since I tell you, it is not easy to practice Buddhism every day and all day! It is an excruciating amount of work required out of a practitioner.

I thought that my mind was overwhelmed with all the teachings that I so far have heard since I arrived here; but now after what *roshi* had said, my mind was racing even more with uncontrollable thoughts. As both of us were walking out from the *zendo* and heading to the garden, I asked my *diadía* (uncle).

"Don't get me wrong, I'm extremely grateful for such profound and meaningful lessons. The only problem that I have is how the heck do I retain it all?

"*Ti chto dúmayesh?* (What do you think?) Is there a way to simplify these lessons that I'm being exposed to in such a short period of time?" I asked him with a desperate look.

The dark sky that was above us didn't have a single star shining, but his glowing smile with the few gold front teeth in his mouth was all we needed to brighten up the night. Him smiling at me meant that he expected to hear me complain, and he was right.

"*Slúshayi ménia*! (Listen to me!) I understand your frustration and how overwhelming it can become from being exposed to so many lessons in a few days.

"Everything that you have heard and learned since you arrived so far are just words. In order for you to feel the results of them you have to apply them to your life on a daily basis; and with time they will become part of your life and guide you throughout your journey.

"*Ti chto za'bil* (Did you forget) how only a few days ago you were in complete distress and knew absolutely nothing about Buddhism? *Nu a seyíchás*, (But now,) not only do you understand the main principles of the practice, but you also managed to bring some peacefulness into your heart. So, give yourself some credit. Besides, no one ever said it will be easy, since an easy path does not change a man for the better, but only for the worse.

"By simply being here you are already making progress in your life. You are already on the right path. The way to change ourselves is through the practice, the practice that you are currently practicing, since it is this practice that causes us to become aware of our adventurous, dangerous, agitated, obsessive behaviors; and in the process expose us to ourselves so that we could tame our negative behaviors.

"Buddha said,
The only way we can find
Peace in our hearts,
Find the pathway

ZEK

That leads to liberation,
Is by changing ourselves
Not by changing the world."

Day IV
Errant Mind

I slept through the night like I was a corpse, not even remembering how I got myself to the bed. But I do remember having a weird dream, like I woke up earlier than usual in the morning with a craving to meditate and be alone; and in my eerie dream I went out of my room into the garden and sat under a tree on the red and yellow leaves out of desperation to bring some peace to my wandering mind; but instead, I found myself lost even more in errant thoughts until I felt something moving by my side in the grass under the red-yellow leaves.

I opened my eyes and saw a black snake crawling next to me. I thought, one wrong, sudden move and that would bring the end to my lonely journey.

I sat alert with eyes wide open and concentrated with all the power of my mind; watching, scolding with my eyes every twisted move that snake was making. Scared I was, but also so wide awake that I understood right there and then how the meditation must be practiced. The snake eventually had crawled away, but not without leaving in me a sense of great awareness.

Just for that short, scary moment I was able to stay focused without any distractions from my errant mind. The same errant mind that I could never escape from, just like my life-long problems that always follow me around like my shadow.

I'm starting to see more clearly now what I couldn't see before, as if my mind was in the clouds all these years. That by trying to avoid talking about my dark past, it would never bring peace to my mind. I have to master my dark past or I will always remain a slave to it; and what better way to do it than being honest with myself.

> My life in the past feels like it was
> A life-long marathon that began way before
> I even knew how to walk;
> For if I knew that I would be running
> A life-long marathon I would've at least
> Prepared myself the best I could.
> For a very long time, I ran aimlessly
> On my lonely path without a purpose,
> Like an errant breeze.
> I ran because that's what everyone else did
> Around me all the time.
> Everyone else ran, and so did I.
> I kept running without understanding the reason why.
> No one asked questions, and neither did I.
> So, I just assumed that there were no answers
> To my errant questions which were always on my mind.
> No one stopped, unless they died,
> And so, I thought if I were to stop
> Then I would also die,
> And so, I continued to run;
> After running the first four without a break,

ARTEM VASKANYAN

I wanted to stop and puke,
Not because I felt sick and worn out,
But because there was no turning back,
No escaping from a path that I
Unwillingly found myself on.
After another four more, at times
My legs were not with me,
And at other times, I was not with them;
But something deep down within me
Kept whispering to my errant mind,
"Finish what you've started,
Or all of this pain and suffering
Will be in vain."
So, I kept going, kept running,
And not out of the desire to go on
And finish what I'd started when I heard
The whisper in my mind,
But out of fear to see myself fail at my goal,
Like many others did around me all the time.
Sometimes there were moments when my errant mind
Was lost like a breeze amongst the trees,
And helpless fallen red-yellow leaves;
I would've stopped a long time ago
If it wasn't for my inner ego,
Who kept pushing me and telling me,
Don't look back!
So, I kept going! And praying!
To whoever was listening to me,
To at least help me finish half.
After two more, I was halfway done,
So, I kept telling myself,
"Do what you did again, one more time!"
I couldn't help myself
But to take my eyes off my path
And look at the prize with all my heart;
Imagining myself arriving to the finish line

ZEK

With cheer in my heart
And joy in my soul,
And yelling fearlessly into the limitless sky,
"I've survived!
Is this the best you can do
To make me suffer like you always do?"
I wanted a taste of what I sowed so bad
That I completely forgot
About my lonely path.
I tried to escape with my errant mind,
But in the end paid for it
With more suffering than I would normally have.
I devoured *vora*ciously unripe fruits
While in my errant mind they were sweet
And juicy when I took a bite.
All of my arduous work
Began to crumble and go to waste,
But when six-and-a-half more went by
In the blink of an eye,
It taught me to cherish every single painful
Moment of my life,
For it is still my life
Regardless how bitter it was.
It was those painful moments from my dark past
That nowadays remind me of who I was once,
And how much I changed into the man that I am today.
And it was those dark, painful moments
That made me realize at the end
That it is only in the dark
That I could see the stars
And the beautiful moon glowing.
It was after my first one-and-a-half
That burned me out so damn bad
That it left me breathless
With both lungs collapsed,
But I kept telling to myself;

"You stop, you die!"
I kept saying these words over and over again,
Until I turned them into a mantra of my own
In my errant mind.
I couldn't tell at first
How strong my life-long marathon had made me,
Not till I saw the others run along with me.
Yes! It is painful, and it is hard!
And it is not for everyone to be a part,
But what choice does any one of us really have
When the life-long trek
Begins to knock on our door
Before we even get a chance
To stand on our own two feet and open the door.
Anyone can start, this much is true,
But only a few can finish.
Starting is the easiest part
It is the middle and towards the end
That is the most difficult to overcome
Before it will come to an end.
When under five was finally left
I could practically taste the prize
At the end of each day in my errant mind.
I kept saying to myself:
"Keep your head straight!
Don't look back!
Don't think of the prize,
Think of the goal instead;
And maybe, just maybe, one day,
I'll cross the finish line
And have a good laugh in front of all of those
Who wished for me to fail
Who threw stones at my feet
Prayed for my demise and spat in my face
When I was down on my knees
Begging for someone to come

ZEK

And treat me like a human being."
But as one path came to an end,
It led me to another, to where now I am.
Who will I become this time,
Once I cross this finish line?
My errant mind cannot help itself
But to wander all the time.

Day V
Great Doubt

"Ever since I can remember I felt like every day was a test that I never knew how to prepare myself for. *Mayá zhízn* (My life) became one big failure, since I failed so many times in life that in the process I completely lost my confidence, that vital consciousness of my power that grows to such magnitude that it would make me believe with every fiber of my body that what I try to do is the correct way.

"But instead of my confidence, I developed great doubt, not only in myself, but in everyone else as well. I used to say to myself, 'Why should I put *mayú véru* (my faith) in someone else's hands and trust their words? What guarantee is there that they aren't looking for a way to deceive me; or that their belief system is the ultimate *právda* (truth)?'

"I grew up in many places as you know, where people *vráli* (lied) through their teeth while looking straight in my eyes; and when someone from time to time did tell *právdu* (the truth) there was no way of knowing; since *právda* and *vran'yó* (the lies) sounded exactly the same; and by the time I could tell the difference between them it was too late, damage was already done.

"I have great doubt that there are people who genuinely help others without a self-interest in mind. Even *manáhi* (monks) who assist others with their teachings to help people find their way in life do so out of self-interest to generate *haróshuyu kármu* (good karma) that would help them reach their enlightenment someday.

"Is it even possible for people to act in unselfish ways? I wonder! *Ésli chésno* (To be frank), I don't think so! I believe we have been created by our God to act with self-interest for a reason, since it is because of our selfishness that we are able to strive and improve ourselves throughout our lives. If there were no reward at the end of our hard work, then there would be no purpose; and *násha daróga k práveshéniyu* (our path to enlightenment) would not exist."

And as I said all of this to my *diadía* as we were on our way to the cafeteria, I noticed how he was nodding his head in agreement and waiting for me to get a breather so he would respond.

"*Ti óchen prável'na rasuzhdáyesh* (You are rationalizing in the right way)," he said. "It is true that the Buddhist practice requires us to seek for answers, and then after finding them have the strength to let them go; and the greater the doubt, the harder the search for answers will be.

> "Buddha said,
> 'Great doubt, great awakening;
> Little doubt, little awakening;
> No doubt, no awakening.'"

As we entered into the cafeteria, we both grabbed our breakfast and sat at the table with other practitioners. We took a few bites of oatmeal with strawberries and my *diadía* continued.

"I, just like you, have doubt. At times my doubt is little, and at times it is great; but I'm never without a doubt. Doubt is what makes me search and look for answers.

"If to every sickness there is a cure, then to every question there must be an answer; and if I cannot find what I'm looking for, then it does not mean that there is no answer. All it means is that I'm searching in the wrong place, asking the wrong questions. The only way to find my answers is for me to continue to search for them, starting with myself, since,

>"The way to the enlightenment
> Is to know myself,
> And to know myself
> I must forget myself,
> And to forget myself,
> I must be enlightened by all things,
> Like Buddha.'"

We left the table and headed to the *zendo*. On the way there my *diadia* continued.

"Forgetting myself has always been the greatest challenge of *mayéyi zhízni* (my life) throughout my practice. To forget myself is to let go of all regrets and mistakes that I had made. I had to completely empty myself so I could start my new path as a reborn person, just like emptying dirty water out of a cup so I could pour a fresh one in.

"It is because of doubt, that lack of confidence in ourselves and *davéria* (trust) in others, that makes us work much harder on our own to discover *právdu* (the truth) we seek. Everything that you have learned since you have started *sesshin*, you have to put it to practice. You have to apply it *k svayéyi zhízni* (to your life) in order to see if it does work. You should never make someone's teachings part of your life without testing them with the clear mind." He finished his last words right before we stopped by the *zendo*.

We both entered and ended up sitting in different places. I ended up sitting somewhere in the middle of the meditation hall while my *diadia* disappeared somewhere in the front row.

ZEK

Day V
An Angry Wasp

I sat motionless, numb to the arising thoughts, surprisingly not caring about how sweet and promising my arising thoughts appeared to be. I managed to find a steady breath which guided me through my meditation. I stared into a space seeing everything and everyone, and at the same time nothing and no one at all. At first, I felt connected with my mind and body until out of nowhere something buzzed over my head, and then again a few times more. It was *asá* (a wasp) for it had a yellow-striped body.

I tried not to pay it any mind, but *asá* kept buzzing over my head and getting closer to me every time. *Mayí glazá* (My eyes) were wide open, looking with peripheral vision, paying close attention to an angry wasp that just wouldn't let me be. It appeared to be trapped in the room as it desperately searched for a way out. A few windows were wide open and *asá* was inches away from its freedom, but it just couldn't see it. No matter how hard it tried to fly from one window to another, it just couldn't see an open window that was right in front of its *glúpayi rózhayi* (dumb face).

From being trapped in the room it grew more aggravated as it noisily flew over our heads. No one seemed to care but me; perhaps because I was the only one with a fear from getting stung by an angry wasp, since from all of the people in the room, for some unknown reason it chose me.

Zláya asá (An angry wasp) zoomed in on me like it declared war against me as it circled around my head like a hawk circles its prey from above before it strikes. As the humming sounds intensified, it began to get closer and closer until it started to attack. I was swaying my head to the sides like *baksyúr* (a boxer) dodges punches, while everyone in the room remained silent, motionless in the meditative state of mind. It seemed as if *zláya asá* gave up on finding its escape to freedom and said, "*Póhuyi!* (Fuck it!) If I'm going to die like a trapped rat, then I might as well take one of these damn humans with me to hell."

I understood exactly how this *zláya asá* felt when it realized that it was trapped because I've seen similar behavior before, only not with a wasp, but with men who were trapped in prison for a very long time without a chance to ever see *svyét* (the light) again. I saw how anger transformed young and old, dumb and intelligent, strong and fragile minds who once were all full of life to walking corpses without a care for their or anyone else's life. When they accepted their defeat, then they began to transform into angry, bitter men and live their lives only with one goal in mind: how to inflict pain and suffering upon those who have a chance to see *svyét* one day. The same souls who were full of life from having a positive energy, who had a way to bring joy and love around the other men and make them feel alive and look forward with excitement to what tomorrow might bring, were now drained out of their own energy, and not only by the long-term imprisonment, but by their own self-defeat; and once that transformation was achieved, then they abandoned all of their moral principles that stood in their way of bringing misery and destruction to other men who strove to stay alive just so they could make themselves feel better at the end of the day.

A chubby guy with a grey beard who was sitting next to me turned and whispered: "Try not to move and it will fly away. Trust me, I know bees! I'm a beekeeper!"

I took his advice, since he sounded like he knew what he was talking about, and so I remained still, and since there was no other better suggestion or any other help coming my way, I gladly took his advice without questioning it.

The whole situation felt like I was playing a game of chess, only this time I was the chess piece sitting in the middle of the game board; and running out of time before my opponent, *zláya asá* (an angry wasp) would put me in a checkmate. In a way, it was like being back *v tyur'mé* (in prison) since

>Life in prison was just like a game of chess,
>Where I was trapped in the same place
>Surrounded by the same people
>Like a chess piece
>Amongst the chess pieces
>On the chess board;
>And every person that I encountered
>Was always face to face,
>Like an opponent in the chess game
>Who meditates on his move long and hard
>Before he moves his piece;
>But,
>The only difference always was
>The price you pay
>When you lose in a game of chess.

And I most definitely didn't want to lose this one to my opponent, the wasp.

Only my eyes were set in motion, moving in every direction within 180 degrees as my body was rooted like a tree in one place; but *tupáya asá* (the stupid wasp) persisted to harass, flying above and around me; but when it landed on my ear, it crossed the line! I, without holding back and with all respect to the First Precept, Not Killing, whacked with all my strength my ear with an open palm. Two loud sounds resonated throughout the meditation hall when I made my move. First, the sound of the whack on my ear by my open palm, which sounded exactly like the *jukpi* when *roshi* whacks it on his open palm to awaken practitioners from the meditative state to bring them back to the present moment. Everyone thought that it was *roshi* who whacked the *jukpi*, as they adjusted themselves to a new position. Even *roshi* himself thought for a second that it was him as he, with a puzzled look and raised eyebrows, looked at both of his hands to see if it was him or not and then checked if his *jukpi* was there by his side and that no one was messing with it; and the second sound was the sound of my yelp when I, out of my anger, managed to yell out, "*Súka!*" ("Bitch!") from being stung by the wasp, who then buzzed off to one of the open windows and disappeared. Good thing that I yelped *po Rúskyi* (in Russian) and not in English, for only a few turned around and gave me a stern look. One of those was my *diadía* whose head I saw popping out from the back row trying to find me with his eyes. I was more angry at the beekeeper than with the wasp. I gave him a stern look for a minute or two without blinking my eyes not even once. It occurred to me that *asá* (a wasp) is not a bee, but who cares what it was or was not, the damage to my ear was done as the fake beekeeper was now sitting quietly pretending not to notice me as I kept staring angrily at him while rubbing my ear with my hand.

    I could feel my ear swelling up, growing larger and larger with every breath I inhaled. I felt as if it was about to explode, and so I got up very silently and left in the middle of meditation. By the time I got to my room, my ear grew twice its usual size; and since I naturally have big ears as it is, it became half the size of my head. As bad as it was, at least I wasn't allergic to the bee, or the wasp, or whatever the heck it was that stung me. After a little while I went back to the *zendo* with the pinching pain in my ear and angry from being stung.

ARTEM VASKANYAN

Day V
Eradicating Negativity

I entered the meditation hall and saw monks and some practitioners prostrating to the Buddha statue. The entire purpose of prostrating is done to show devotion and respect to our own innate *Buddha-nature*, the true unchanging and eternal nature of all beings that possesses the seeds of *Buddhahood*, the awakened mind; and also to show to ourselves that we (the practitioners) have the potential to become enlightened like *Buddha*. It also serves a role of eradicating out of ourselves the feeling of pride; and promotes mental and spiritual discipline in the practice. Practicing prostration in the Buddhist practice is not easy to adapt to for many practitioners, since it requires us to embarrass ourselves by getting down on both knees in the presence of many and bow several times to the Buddha statue and elder monks during services. It particularly can be difficult for the Westerners to perform because culturally and traditionally they are different from the Oriental concepts of demonstrating homage and politeness to the elders and icons and holy symbols such as *Buddha* statues.

As I sat down, the monks began to chant a mantra; Om…a two-syllable word, holding the sound for a lingering moment and at the same time exhaling it; and then, repeating it all over again. I was told that the purpose of reciting mantras was to sow merits and wisdom, and at the same time eradicate evil *karma*.

Together with the monks I hummed the lingering sound of the Om…, and as the sound vibrated throughout my mind, I began to feel calm to the point that I completely forgot about an angry wasp and an enlarged ear that hung on the side of my head. The last harmonious sound of the Om… dissipated at the end of the meditation hall with a distant echo; and then, suddenly followed by the cracking sounds from the *jukpi* made by *roshi* as he, after a long pause, began to speak.

"Once hateful thoughts arise and we continue to hang on to them, we then open a door and welcome hate into our hearts; and as hate begins to dwell within our hearts, anger floods our minds with thoughts of violence and revenge.

"Consequently, these negative emotions begin to consume us and spread within us like a disease, like cancer spreads through flesh and rots the bones to their core; and in the process destroys our spiritual growth along with every positive deed that took a lifetime for us to cultivate. All good that we had managed to accomplish for ourselves would be all gone, replaced by the negativity that we had indulged ourselves on.

"Generating good *karma* through positive deeds is only half the work. Keeping them is completely another.

"Those who caused us harm deserve our pity and forgiveness, and not our hate and revenge. If their minds were only clear, free from hateful thoughts, then they would've known the pain and suffering that their wicked actions were doing to us.

"If they only were awakened out of their ignorance, then they would've never even dared to raise an evil thought, never mind to even cause harm to others.

"If we continue to indulge in hatred and seek vengeance, then we will continue to suffer; and if we don't resist the anger and the negative emotions that arise with it, then hate will consume our minds; and we will repeat the same hateful acts against others as it has been done against us; and in the end, we will be no different from any of those who harmed us and poisoned our minds with their wicked acts. If we give in to this evil, then it will transform us into the same wicked beings that we despise and criticize so much; ultimately, we will hate ourselves because we will become just like them.

"Compassion is the antidote to every negative emotion that we find ourselves battling with. Compassion will generate within us a necessary inner strength to help us overcome what we despise. Without compassion in our lives, anger will continue to spread like a wildfire and destroy every positive thought and poison our minds like the water in the well is poisoned by the venomous snake that dwells there.

"By cultivating compassion, it will gradually alleviate our inner pain and in the process eradicate negativity like unwanted weeds in the garden being pulled out one at a time, until they eventually are all gone; and when they are gone it will lessen our suffering and reward us with pleasingly beautiful flowers, bringing us peace and happiness to our lives.

"To cultivate compassion requires us to involve ourselves in helping those in need, protect the weak, and guide the ignorant with our enlightened teachings. However, the latter part requires us first to attain some wisdom, since wisdom allows us to further expand our understanding in how and why suffering occurs; and understand that all sentient beings strive toward happiness; and that sometimes they just do not know how to achieve inner happiness without causing harm to others.

"By chasing our happiness at the expense of others' happiness will only generate more of the negative *karma* within us, consequently leading us to become even more ignorant and angry at life, especially when we do not get what we desire.

"Understanding not only how all human beings function, but also how all beings are related to each other. This will make us realize that hostile actions and words only prolong suffering and creates further distance for us to attain positive *karmic* qualities.

"With wisdom, compassion can be practiced at a much deeper spiritual level, since once wisdom is applied to the practice of compassion, it has the power to purify the heart and heal the soul just like the land filters the rainwater and heals the earth. Thus, ultimately, giving us strength to eradicate negative thoughts from which everything else arises."

Day V
Two Kinds

It was almost afternoon when I returned to my room after the morning practice. I laid down to rest to decompress from the teachings as I rubbed my ear to help alleviate the pain; but it wasn't long till my mind was stormed with thoughts from the past, reminding me when I was finally released from prison, and where my first few weeks as a free man I spent my time with *mayéyi stárayi bratvóyi* (my old brotherhood) trying to catch up on lost years; but no matter how much I tried to fill an empty void in my heart, at the end of each night I felt as I was living in a dream that reminded me of the past that I could never return to.

Looking at my *bratvá* (brotherhood) as they were drinking themselves to the point of total oblivion and throwing dollar bills at *gólim shlyúham* (the naked whores) made me ask myself, what am I doing here? I realized then that whatever I once had in common with *mayéyi bratvóyi* (my brotherhood) and the lifestyle that I once shared with them, those days were long gone. The thing was that once a person's heart changes and breaks away from the crippled mentality, he would not crave to return to his old ways. It is the same as when a man achieves enlightenment then going back to ignorance no longer becomes desirable. I thought that I missed it all, but I didn't. *Ésli skazát právdu* (To tell the truth), I couldn't even look at them, since so many years had passed, and yet they have remained unchanged. Never evolved into someone better. It was sad in a way to see grown-ass men act like *durakí* (fools). Life is all about learning, changing yourself for the better, and just simply evolving out of the self-destructive ways; but to always stay in the same frame of mentality that is just beyond being *gloóp'im* (a fool).

Perhaps I belonged with them once, but after years of being alone, these people that I at some point called *mayími druz'yámi* (my friends) are now complete strangers to me, since they were wasting their precious time. The time that I learned to value with my life when I desperately waited for my moment to be released. So, I would fulfill my dreams and make something out of *mayéyi zhízni* (my life). I spent too many years waiting for that moment, and now that it had finally arrived, I was squandering my precious time with these *nyeudáchnikami* (losers) and licentious *zhénshinami* (women) who don't care about no one but the dollar bills.

I felt disgusted and not with them, but with myself, since it was I who found myself back in the same place that I swore to myself to never return to again. Being there with them reminded me of when I was in my prison cell standing in front of my window during my sleepless nights; and looking at *pólnuyu lunú* (the full moon) as I was begging God to give me strength to survive another night and let me see the sky from outside these prison walls one day.

I had to get up and leave these selfish, lewd people, these walls that were suffocating me, and this noise that was aggravating me. I felt like I was back in prison surrounded by the ignorant who all they did was yell, get high off *narkatyé* (drugs) and drunk off *bukhlá* (booze); but only this time I had a choice. I could get up and leave and never return to this soul-wrecking life again.

ZEK

Many think that the reason for prison being a dehumanizing place is because of the cold, dark, isolated cells, the fences with barbed wires, the walls and towers around the prison yard, when in fact it is the people who turn it into that disgusting, inhumane place with all their rules and immoral behaviors.

When I looked around the room while I was getting a lap dance, deep down in my heart I felt as if all of my *bratvá* that I loved and respected all of my young years were not the people who I thought they were. I don't even think they knew who they were, since I haven't seen too many of them end up and try to survive in a place like I had; and not just survive, but also manage to preserve one's moral principles intact. Many men managed to survive the prison life but only a few did it with dignity; and so, I asked myself while *shlyúha* (a whore) was giving me a lap dance, who would they become once this warm, cozy, friendly, and loving place would be taken from them and replaced with a hell-like place surrounded by the barbed wire fences and 25-foot high walls with electric wires, and instead of beautiful *zhénshin* (women) replaced with *pídarami* (the chicken hawks/queers) armed with knives who chase young men who wouldn't stand up for themselves, and not for *déngi* (money), but for their *zhópu* (ass). What kind of *zek* (a convict) will they turn into? Will the little guy become *pahanóm* (boss) or will the big guy turn into *tyurémskuyu súku* (a prison bitch); and since I have seen where the size of *muzhiká* (a man) did not matter, since if *zek* has no *sérdza* (heart) then no matter where he ends up, he will always suffer, mostly by his own hand.

I couldn't help myself but to judge everyone from a cynical point of view, as my eyes circled around the room like a hawk from above looking for his prey; and in the process creating imaginary scenes and placing each one of them in a different situation where they would have to reveal the true essence of their hearts; but the truth was that I already knew what each one of them stood for. Just by looking at the way they talked, laughed, and walked, I had an answer.

One thing that I had mastered *v tyur'mé* (in prison) was how to be a good judge of character. *Mayá zhízn* (my life) depended on being careful around people. I knew I wasn't *v tyur'mé*, and yet, I couldn't help myself but to keep seeing the world from a confined cell. It was like looking through a magical lens that revealed to me the depths of the person's spirits.

As I was sitting on the sofa with *krasívayi bábayi* (a beautiful broad) by my side, I remembered what my *bábushka* (grandmother) used to say to me when I was a young kid:

> "In this world,
> There are only two kinds of human beings,
> The good and the wicked.
> The good are calm and peaceful
> In their minds and spirits,
> While the wicked are loud, flashy, and scandalous.
> If you find a person with a wicked soul,
> And with that person you feel comfortable
> To share your life with,
> Then your soul is just as wicked
> As it is with whom you chose
> To share your life with.
> For the soul attracts what it desires,
> And what it desires is
> A soul who is just like yours."

Just like yours… just like yours… just like yours… Her last words were ringing in my head until I got up and left the room without looking back, leaving everyone perplexed and with raised eyebrows. But I didn't care! I just kept walking away from everyone.

Day V
Inferno

(It all starts with an evil seed
Being planted in a pure heart
By those who succumb to the wicked deed
From an angry mind.
The seed resides quietly within,
Until one day,
The negative emotions begin to arise
From a single evil thought
That pollutes a peaceful mind.
The mind is weak, confused, and lost.
It can't let go of an evil thought.
An evil seed begins to sprout

Faster than it was at first devoured.
Its roots extend its poison
Reaching deep down into the essence
Of its heart,
Where it ignites the burning flames of fire,
And begins to spread faster than
A living, breathing wildfire;
And there in the midst of it all
Where anger arises and dwells,
It can never be destroyed,
But only tamed like the mind
We can barely control.
It tricks the mind with a promise,
If only it would let it have
Its vengeance,
Then it would extinguish the flames of fire,
And ease the burning flame of pain
That dwells within, inferno.
But instead, it devours
All the good that it can
When it visits the hearts of others,
Just like once it was done to mine.)

That night I slept like a log consumed in a ruminating dream until I was awakened by the thunderous sounds of the lightning. I tried to fall back to sleep, but thunder persisted to keep me awake throughout the night. An unpleasant feeling arose within me, and I felt like there was a stone in my heart that I didn't know how to extract. I do not care what anyone says, but you just don't forget the lingering, torturous years of *tyurémskayi zhízni* (prison life). You just cannot get rid of the internal pain caused by so many years from living in isolation and despair. The feeling of constant pain and loneliness that had been etched into my memory doesn't allow me to let go. I couldn't see the side effects of *tyurémskayi zhízni* while I was still living there; but now that I'm no longer there, I see how it left me in so much pain that a simple thought of it begins to drain my body out of energy. It puts me in such a crippled state of mind where all of the negative emotions suddenly arise within me all at the same time; and when that happens, I start to feel like *mayá zhízn* (my life) is coming to an end; then my trepidation suddenly begins; and then,

> I cannot think, talk, nor listen,
> My mind gets lost, confused,
> And it gets harder and harder to breathe.
> I'm choking, hyperventilating, dazed.
> I'm gasping for air more and more…
> I cannot breathe!
> I feel trapped!
> The walls are closing in on me,
> I'm suffocating!
> I panic!
> I'm sweating profusely,
> My heartbeat beats faster and faster, louder
> My blood runs faster through my veins.
> I see a total darkness in my eyes.
> I'm drowning!
> In the middle of the lake.
> I scream for help!
> But I'm too far away from the shore
> For any soul to hear my cry;
> And at the end of my trepidation,
> All I feel is anger
> From being helpless, abandoned, and alone.

I used to ask myself during many sleepless *nacheyí* (nights), what is worse, *smyért' ili tyurmá* (death or prison)? And for a very long time my answer always was *tyurmá*, since for me it was the real inferno where on my worst days I would feel as if the heart of my soul was burning.

It was like being in a coma where I wasn't dead nor alive, and on the days when I would be discouraged to fight for myself so I could ameliorate the essence of my soul, I then would feel as if I was losing the last fray for my mind, body, and soul.

Part of me wants to let go of these painful thoughts and finally be free from them all once and for all, while the other part wants to hold on and remember that wretched *zhízn* (life), as if it wants me to come back to misery. To a place where I fought every day to preserve my sanity along with my humanity.

The more I ruminated as I paced back and forth in my room, the more I felt my heart rising up into my throat, eyes widening, teeth grinning, hands trembling. It was the same exact feeling that I had on the first day when I ended up in *tyur'mé* (prison) when I was thrown into an isolated, dark, cold *klétku* (cell) on the first day of my arrest, where I spent several weeks without sunlight, shower, a phone call to my *mátushka* (mother), and fresh air, since the window in my *klétki* (cell) was deliberately welded shut and painted over with black paint; and the light beam on the ceiling was always on from six in the morning till midnight, keeping me awake; and I remember myself pacing back and forth in my tiny *klétki* for as long as the lights stayed on; and the whole entire time I would pray and beg *Bóga* (God) to let me out of this damn hole, out of this living, breathing inferno that is burning in the heart of my soul.

I became engulfed even further by my thoughts; but I didn't mind for I had a goal in mind: to dig as much as I possibly could within the depths of my *dushí* (soul) to help me understand myself even deeper.

At the beginning of my prison sentence I was lost, confused, and without guidance. I worked with the tools just like other *zéki* (convicts) acquired throughout their lives, which in my case were not a lot. Only enough, though, to make me fit in amongst other *varóv* (thieves), but not amongst those who desperately tried to find their way out of the suffering and their old ways of life which led them just like the rest of us to end up where we all were in the first place. It makes sense now why they isolated themselves from the rest of *zékav* (cons) like me, since it is impossible to transform one's life for the better by continuing to be around negativity. It is important to understand that if your goal is to improve your life, then you have to learn how to isolate yourself from the negative people. Otherwise, you will be going in circles without making any progress in your *zhízni* (life).

Back then I used to make fun of them, and even had a name for them, *chudachkí* (weirdos); but who knew that down the road I would become one of them, completely isolating myself from the rest of my fellow *varóv v zakónye* (thieves in law) in hopes to ameliorate my life just like those *chudachkí* were doing.

What gave me an inspiration to gradually withdraw myself from *varóv v zakónye* was because of one particular *starichók* (little old man) who had been in *tyur'mé* (prison) for over 40 years, an incomprehensible number of years that he was sentenced to by the so-called "justice system." He ended up in *tyur'mé* at a very young age just like I was, but managed to find his spiritual path and persevere, despite living in such a soul-depriving place. He stood out for me amongst everyone else that I've met in *tyur'mé* because of what he had once said to me. It was a short proverb that became etched into the back of my mind:

> "If you keep looking back
> Then you'll miss all your life
> Ahead of you."

It was these words of wisdom that motivated me to start taking advantage of my time in *tyur'mé* because when I heard them it scared me out of my mind. I understood at least this much, that if I were to continue to dwell on my past, then I would prolong my suffering and fuel my anger. I would become trapped within my own mind, reliving every awful moment of *mayéyi zhízni* (my life) and missing a chance to have a happy future. I felt as if the rest of *mayéyi zhízni* depended on me to grasp that what I did or didn't do in the past, it simply didn't matter, since I had no control over it; but what did matter is what I do with my life now, since it will determine the outcome of the rest of *mayéyi zhízni*.

The worst thing that any *zek* (convict) can do while being in *tyur'mé* (prison) is to waste his time and then go home empty handed. What I mean by that is, when *zek* serves his entire tyuremskiyi srok (prison sentence), and during his time in *tyur'mé* he learns absolutely nothing that he could utilize to improve his *zhízn* (life) once he is released; whether it is acquiring a skill to help him with work down the road, or understanding a little more about himself and the mistakes that he had made which led him to end up in *tyur'mé*, or simply persevere in some way or another; thus when *zek* fails to achieve the minimum of these obligations, then he had been robbed of his precious time not once, but twice. The first, by the prison system, and the second, by his own making when he chose not to take advantage of his precious time, the opportunity to transform his life's misfortunes into some success, but instead wasting it on doing nothing but growing bitter and angry while awaiting helplessly for his release, if he even has one.

The hardest part for me at first was to understand the importance of time. That time was not on my side, and the more I grappled with myself internally, the more *yá pónil* (I understood) that it would be a disgrace to waste my time in a place where all I had was time, and not make any progress out of it; then that would've been the greatest loss of *mayéyi zhízni* (my life).

This was exactly what *starichók* (little old man) was implying to me. Do as much as you possibly can while there is still time; and don't let the past dictate over your future, since dwelling on it would only perpetuate the inner suffering. *Starochók* had to forget himself, empty his mind completely in order to start rebuilding himself as a new person; and not just with an intent to survive *tyurémskuyu zhízn* (prison life), but to genuinely change his inner self. All that pollution that he must've inhaled throughout his life prior to committing his crime had to be eradicated. He understood that, and because of that dedicated his *zhízn* (life) to cultivating his *Buddha-nature*.

Over time my goal in *tyur'mé* became the same as it did for *starichók*. To attain *Buddhahood* through cultivating my *Buddha-nature* and one day look in the mirror with my head held high, and say to myself:

"I like who you're becoming!"

But that didn't exactly happen to me. At least not to the level that I wanted it to be. I strived to improve myself even more, but I seemed to reach my plateau, and didn't know how to surpass it, since I kept using the same tools that led me to my demise over and over again in hopes to get a different result; and with time as I found better tools, they only got me so far, that I felt like I was going in circles like a lost *barán* (sheep) without a pastor, not understanding the real reason for my confusion. However, my determination to change for the better never diminished, instead it only became greater throughout my time in *tyur'mé* (prison); and ever since I discovered within myself the potential to grow, I never stopped carrying that flame in my heart that insatiably craves to expand my intellect and become better as a human being.

I must admit it was not easy to transform my corrupt mindset into a purer version of me, especially after everything that was taught to me by my family and *bratvóyi* (brotherhood) since I was young. But like my *diadía* said, "An easy way does not make a man great! It is only the difficult path that makes a man fulfill his goal to the fullest." And the more I rewired myself from my old ways of thinking that I learned to do by heart, the more I began to detest that old way of life.

Nevertheless, as much as I wholeheartedly despised that place that I often called a living, breathing inferno, where I endured all kinds of hardships; from unbearable freezing to hot temperatures; from hunger to total isolation and loneliness; from manipulative and cunning individuals who preyed on the weak; and from constant despair of losing my *mátushka* and even at times the presence of *Bóga* (God). As bad as that place was, I cannot deny the fact that it was also a place where I have molded myself into the man that I'm today. That place became a polishing stone and I that impure gem, where for many lingering years all I did was polish myself against it until I got rid of as many impurities as I possibly could.

After some time, I started to look at the prison not as the inferno, but as an institution where I could learn about life. I would look at it as a college for *zékav* (prisoners). It was there where I learned how to stand up for my beliefs; appreciate every little good deed that came my way; fight with all of my conviction every battle to the end like there was no tomorrow; and never, ever give up no matter how difficult my path was. For me, to give up meant to die, and dying was not an option.

Believe it or not, there were moments when I slept in *tyur'mé* (prison) better than I do now while I'm *svabodyén* (free); and there were many sleepless nights like the one I'm having now when I felt like I was the only living being in this cruel, unjust world who understood the true pain from being alone. I miss those soulful moments. I wish at times that I could reconnect with my inner self more often so I could bring out of me that fighting *dúh* (spirit) that conquers new challenges with conviction. I miss old me! The old me that did everything like it was between *zhízni yí smérti* (life and death).

As difficult as it might be for some to understand
That at times I'm truly grateful
For some of those soul-depriving times;
For they had made me understand
What needs to be done to mold myself
Into a man that I have strived
For so long to become.
For it was during those lingering, dark years
That I made a choice of who I wanted
And didn't want to be;
And now, all I'm doing
Is pursuing the same path
That I had chosen intuitively
Long before I even knew
That I would even try to pursue;
In a place that I often call
The living, breathing inferno.

For *zékav* (prisoners) who had all the support that they needed from their family and friends, their time in *tyur'mé* (prison) was completely different from mine. It was less lonely for them, and most importantly, they had the financial support from their loved ones once they were released from prison; but in my case, I had none, and since I expected nothing from no one, including from my *diadía* (uncle) who disappeared after my *mátushka* (mother) passed away, including those so-called *bratvá* (brotherhood) who never even wrote me a single letter, nor supported me in any kind of way, nor even helped my *mátushka* when she became ill. All of this taught me a valuable lesson, making me realize that no one will ever help unless there is something in it for them; and it was because of that self-awareness that I started to work extra hard on myself. I pushed myself to learn as much as I could like my life depended on it because it absolutely did. I wanted to leave *tyur'mú* (prison) with something that I could apply to my life and not be lost and confused and traumatized by *tyurémskayi zhízni* (the prison life). Well, the latter part didn't exactly happen for me. I failed on that part miserably. Nevertheless, everything positive that I did manage to achieve was on my own, although I wish that I had a teacher to guide me throughout those years, for I would've accomplished much greater things. I wish that I would've had someone like my *díadía*, but I didn't. Instead, all I had was me and my ravaged *sérdzye* (heart). But at least I know that I did everything in my power that I could to benefit from that dark, and at the same time, enlightening place.

I don't know what it was that triggered this unpleasant, and at the same time, enlightening feeling in me. Was it *zláya asá* (the angry wasp) or from ruminating on my dark past? One thing that my thoughts do reveal to me is that I always thought that *tyur'má* (the prison) was a place of inferno, but now I'm not so sure, since now I realize that it was not a place but more like a state of mind; since I can't dispute the fact that I'm in a place of peace and calm, love, compassion, and guidance, and yet at times, I feel like there is a living, breathing inferno in my chest ready to explode.

Day VI
The Path to Buddhahood

I suddenly woke up gasping for air in the midst of the night. My clothes were drenched in sweat from a nightmare before the dawn even appeared on the horizon. A long, unpleasant memory, that's all it was. I had hoped it was long forgotten and overcome within these few days, but it was not. Instead, it came back out of the blue, and with a guilty feeling in my heart from not visiting my *mátushka* (mother) in a very long time. For a minute there I was in a comatose state, confused and trying to figure out where I exactly was, and as I was about to get dressed and go and see her, it dawned on me that she had been long gone for many years now. Right there and then I realized how much I've missed her. I wish I would've appreciated every happy and sad moment that I had with her even more when we were together and apart.

ZEK

As I laid in bed ruminating on my past, a sudden, awkward, and at the same time, enlightening feeling arose within me to remind me of one of the teachings of the *Buddha*. The part that refers to letting go of all of the judgmental thoughts. I knew if I were to persist in indulging on my unpleasant memories that anger, hatred, and revenge will storm my mind once again. Every time when my memories of the past *zhízni* (life) return to me it would bring with it these self-destructive thoughts, and in particular, the loathing that I have for my mother's neglect. It had stayed with me ever since I was young. I tried so many times to let it go even when she was still *zhiváya* (alive), but when she unexpectedly passed away, she also left this sickening feeling in my heart. I still grieve, since I never had a chance to properly say to her *prasháyi* (goodbye), not like a son should have with his dying *mátushka*.

Every time I think of her, I start to feel like there is a piece of ice lodged in my heart. Is it even possible to let it go when all I feel deep within my heart is hurt? It's like these disturbing memories had bound themselves within my *dushoyi* (soul).

> I've tried so many times,
> In so many ways,
> In so many places,
> To let it all go.
> That I'm starting to highly doubt
> That letting go isn't possible without forgiving,
> And forgiving isn't possible without forgetting,
> And forgetting isn't possible,
> Unless the mind is completely erased;
> And is that even possible?
> I wonder!

I rose from the bed, threw a robe over me, and went out of my room for an early stroll. On a cold wooden floor bare footed, I quietly paced down the hallway like *prízrak* (a ghost). I tried not to make any noise, but the squeaky wooden floor chirped like a canary with each step. Good thing that no one was awakened by these sounds, for I know that I would've been easily awakened, since I'm a light sleeper.

As I wandered through the empty hallways under the dimmed lights of the candles set along the walls, I noticed a light at the end of the hallway escaping through the cracks of the slightly closed door. The door was open wide enough for me to see inside that it was a place of study of some sort. I stopped and entered into the room. It was the monks' *bibliatéka* (library). It was filled with myriad books and at each round table there were a couple of *manáhov* (monks) sitting, immersed in their studies.

Throughout my stay at the monastery, all I saw was how *manáhi* (monks) diligently dedicated themselves to their practice. They never wasted time. Everything they did was efficient and with precision, whether it was chanting, meditating, gardening, cleaning, or studying, everything they did was to perfection, as if with these activities they were taming their minds. From their point of view, they were running out of time, since *zhízn* (life) is just too short to be wasting time on activities that won't bring peace and calm to the errant mind.

Buddhist monks believe that the only path that can lead to the *Buddhahood*, the awakened mind (the enlightenment), is a peaceful mind. A mind that is not dragged by the body; that is unclouded and in accord with the heart of a good nature; a mind that is free from ignorance; and since negative emotions and delusions constantly take rise from the wicked seeds that had been sowed within us by the ignorant ones; and then prolonged and further cultivated by our own incomprehension, thus, every living being is responsible to tame his own restless mind and find his own path to the *Buddhahood*.

When I entered into *bibliatéku* (the library) at such an unusual early hour, all of the monks stopped at once what they were doing; and stared awkwardly at me for a brief moment. I suppose it was understandable why they were all surprised to see me, since the rest of the practitioners were all sound asleep, and it appeared that I was the only one who was wandering in the hallways like *prízrak* (a ghost). My unexpected visit invoked a great deal of curiosity in one of the elder monks. He wore geeky round glasses that covered most of his round face. He must've been a librarian for he looked like he'd read all of the books.

"Ahhh! What brings you here so early?" he asked as he approached and bowed.

"A nightmare, I suppose," I responded wearily, looking around the room and quickly bowed back.

"Ahhh! I haven't had one of those since I became a monk," he said smiling.

"I'm happy for you!" I said with an intent to put an end to such an early conversation that was starting to annoy me, since all I wanted to do was to clear my head with a quiet stroll. Besides, I haven't even had my cup of coffee yet, nor good sleep in some time; but I did ask for it, since it was I who entered into his domain.

Standing in the middle of the library amongst myriad books and around a dozen *manáhov* made me remember how I used to always spend an extra hour at the library *v tyur'mé* (in prison) so I could quietly read and write my poetry. *Bibliatéka* was a place of sanctuary for me. A place where I could rest my mind and gather my thoughts, and this place reminded me how much I missed it. I looked around the room one more time with a sigh and quietly started to wander off towards the door. The monk with the geeky round glasses never took his eyes off me, watching me closely as he was trying to read me like one of his books; and as I was walking away, "Ahhh! You are already enlightened!" he said enthusiastically, as the rest of the monks dropped what they were doing and all looked at me trying to figure me out.

"Ahhh!" I said and stopped, turned, and looked at him with a perplexed look, squinting my eyes, demanding an explanation.

"You already possess *Buddhahood*, since when you start to acknowledge the inner change within you from your arising thoughts, then you are being aware of what is happening within your mind.

"Your mind might not be perfectly enlightened due to inexperience with the practice, which is why delusions and nightmares continue to arise…"

"But how do I do that? How do I forget! Forgive! And erase the past that keeps dragging me down and taking me off my path?" I asked with a desperate look in my eyes.

"Ahhh! Excellent question, and the answer is… you absolutely don't! All you have to do is to continue to be conscious of your arising thoughts and of all things around you. From things that cause you suffering to things that bring you joy. Being enlightened is being awake, and when you are awake, then all of those self-destructive thoughts that constantly arise and drag you down will dissipate over time with practice.

"Your awareness will give you an ability to recognize all of these internal and external pains and sufferings that are occurring in your life and then understand how to let them go before they even begin to gnaw at you."

"According to the *Buddha*:
'The path to *Buddhahood*
Is to know yourself;
To know yourself
Is to forget yourself;
To forget yourself
Is to erase your mind;
To erase your mind
Is to be enlightened by all things.'"

Day VI
The Lonely Path

It was the cold breeze that woke me up and not the usual sound of the morning gong. I didn't get much sleep that night, yet my thirst for what the sixth day might bring gave the necessary strength to fully stay awake and go outside. That early morning the weather was magnificent. The cool air was thin and crisp, and every breath that I inhaled felt as if it was a new breath of life. The sea of clouds along the mountains' humps stood still as they were trapped, but then gradually began to descend as the sunlight continued to warm the land.

After a short while I heard the sounds of the gong and went inside the housing to the *zendo*. It was a short meditation followed by the *dharma* (Buddhist teachings) talk on loneliness. Hearing about the loneliness made me feel like being alone and to go far away from everyone.

The breakfast is the best meal of the day, at least for me, and I was really looking forward to having the blackberry jam with my pancakes; but it quickly ran out because of one particularly big, fat guy who ate like *kashalót* (a sperm whale). That is not the first time when he doubled up on blackberry jam and then went for seconds. Anyhow, I left a little disappointed and headed to the garden so I could be finally alone.

By the time I got out of the house, the giant fog had descended from the top of the mountains. It covered the monastery like a snow blanket. The hazy cloud was all I could see in front of me. I felt its mugginess on my skin and its moisture in my lungs. I closed my eyes for there was not much to see but the blur all around me; and as I stood still, I subliminally thought of *roshi*'s words when he said:

"Loneliness is the only real thing that I carry with me throughout my life. Loneliness is a part of me, and it will never part from me. It was with me in the past. It is with me now. And it most definitely will be with me in the future and till the end of my days; and even then, will it part from me then?"

I stood and ruminated heavily on his words and somehow felt like I was transported to the top of the highest mountain where I stood on one of its humps and was looking down below. In my mind's eye, I clearly saw the evergreen forest stretch out endlessly into the horizon as far as my eyes could take me; and there amongst the forest in leaves here and there were trees of red and yellow leaves surrounding the monastery.

Nothing around me or within me made any noise. Silence was all I heard. I felt as I was a single bamboo in the midst of the forest standing and swaying gently side to side from a gentle breeze that laid upon me. I felt alone like there was no one else left alive in this world but me and the lonely path ahead of me.

> Alone I came into this unknown world
> Innocent and pure, and...
> Uncorrupt, unenchanted, and free from all--
> Wicked deeds, human greed, worldly attachments,
> And insatiable desires along with all the filth
> That a human heart attracts, accumulates, and holds within.
> Loved I felt unconditionally and strongly wanted,

ZEK

At the beginning;
But it wasn't long
Till love turned to hate, and then…
Abandoned, discarded like a leper
I suddenly felt.
When those who brought me into light
Now showed me darkness,
And their wicked hearts
Were suddenly revealed to me.
Confused, lost, and all alone I soon was,
Not knowing the true reason
For my demise.
Thus, it wasn't long till I began
To transform into what I abhorred
With all my heart right from the start;
And just like that!
I found myself walking on the wrong path
Without feeling a drop of guilt
From being even more corrupt
Than those who left me all alone
On my lonely path;
But all it was the human nature
To love, to hate, and then
Abruptly leave behind.
What will it take for me to see, I wonder!
That alone I will always be,
No matter how much I hide
Behind those so-called friends and family.
I always knew deep down in my heart
How lonely I was,
But never thought that I will always be—
Perhaps, because I was too scared
To admit the truth,
That the only thing in life
Was and is, and always will be real,
The lonely path that I now see

In front of me.
If only I could've seen the truth
Right from the start,
Then I wouldn't have had to endure
All of that unnecessary pain and suffering;
And I would've tried much harder
To stay on the lonely path,
Instead of taking the shortcut
That led me to the godforsaken path.

Day VI
Vagabond

After my wonderment, I began my walking meditation strolling into the heart of the forest. I followed the same narrow path that I've already discovered during my stay here and was quite acquainted with it. The residue from the morning mist was still lingering on the leaves of trees and bushes, and on the long blades of grass as they made my feet wet from wearing sandals as I walked.

Ah! How I love this smell! The smell of the forest. A clean, crisp air entering my lungs. It reminds me of home, of a small village where I grew up as a kid living in a small wooden cabin where we didn't have much. We had no electricity, no running water, and my *mátushka* didn't even work. She didn't need to. Everything that we needed to live comfortably we had on our land. A small farmhouse with a few dozen chickens and ducks that gave us plenty of eggs and poultry, half a dozen goats whose milk we used to make goat cheese, and a cow by the name of Masha that I would milk to fill the whole bucket with milk each morning, and that wasn't it. We had so much land on our farm that we always had fresh *óvashi yi frúkti* (vegetables and fruits). My favored fruit tree was a walnut tree that stood in the middle of our farm. It must've been at least a hundred feet high; and by the end of each season, I would gather tens of huge bags all filled with walnuts that we would sell to our neighbors. And by our wooden cabin we had a gazebo that was covered by the grapevines and whose grapes not only did we eat, but also made *vinó* (wine) out of, which I would steal from the basement once it was fully fermented to get drunk with my *drooz'yámi* (friends).

I must admit life back then was good, although I didn't see it that way when I lived there with my *mátushka*. I always dreamed of getting out of that place that I often called *dermóvaya d'ira* (shithole), telling my *mátushka* that *zhízn v górade* (life in the city) would make our lives better. As I reflect on my life, I come to realize that I had all I needed to be happy. That happiness was always in my life, but I just couldn't see it. Something inside of me just kept pushing me to move away from that beautiful and calm place. It was like I was blind, although I saw clearly, but only the wrong things in life. The things that only the wicked part of my soul craved.

It was my life's misfortunes that made me realize how good things were back then. It's crazy how I blamed everyone around me for causing me grief and pain, but never held myself responsible for my own wicked actions that brought most of my pain to me and upon my own *mátushka*, since both of our lives eventually started to turn to *gavnó* (shit) once we moved into the city, all because I couldn't appreciate what I had.

I guess blaming others for my misfortunes can only go so far before it starts to sound like I'm whining; and then the only thing left for me to say to myself is, do I want some cheese with that whine? Cheese or no cheese, it is I who ultimately holds the power to choose who I want to be as a person at the end of the day. I guess it just doesn't matter anymore who I once was as a person. It is who I am now, at this moment, that matters.

I came to the crossroads where a road to the left was leading me up the hill to the mountain, the other down the hill, and the third straight ahead. My feet were exhausted from walking on the rocky road, especially having small rocks getting stuck inside those sandals, making it harder for me to walk. I chose to go straight ahead, perhaps because I saw my favored flowers up ahead. The lilac's aromatic smell was so fragrant that I almost ate a flower when I ripped the stem of lilac flowers off the bush and rubbed it between my palms to bring the scent into my hands and then rubbed the oil of the flowers on the side of my neck like a cologne.

I walked with butterflies landing on my head and kept my eyes out for angry bees and wasps. I walked until the road got even wider and I no longer had to look down at my feet to stumble on the rocks and slip off the path. Straight ahead of me I noticed a figure of a man heading towards me, and as we both got closer, I could see that it was *staríchók* (an old man) and not *manáh* (a monk), nor a practitioner like me. He walked calmly and with a conviction like the path that he was on belonged to him.

As he approached even closer, I could see that he was a wanderer, a vagabond to be exact, who travels from place to place without a real purpose. I always admired vagabonds, since I often dreamed of becoming one myself when I was trapped *v tyur'mé* (in prison) like *sériyi volk* (a grey wolf) in a cage. Vagabonds are the only people who are free in this world, since they get to roam throughout unknown lands, and I always envied them for that.

"*Namaste*! What a beautiful day!" he said, holding his palms together vertically by his chest and bowed.

"*Namaste*! Oh yeah! It's a great day to be outside," I responded and bowed back.

"Every day is a good day to be out, even when it rains," he said joyfully.

"So, where are you heading?" I asked without thinking it through.

"Wherever my path will lead me! And you?"

"Me! I'm just searching for the right path, I guess!"

"Ha!" he exclaimed with a smirk and said, "There is no such thing as a right or wrong path. There is simply just a path. And whatever it is that you decide to do on that path, whether it is right or wrong, is what will become of it."

"Oh! I never looked at it from this perspective. That kind of makes sense," I said, nodding my head in agreement and added, "So, how is the life of a vagabond nowadays?"

"Funny, no one ever asked me that before, and I met lots of people throughout my journey as a wanderer! Well, I guess…

>Being a vagabond comes with a great sacrifice.
>Just like any good or wicked deed
>Doesn't occur without giving up a part of yourself.
>If people would've sacrificed
>A brief moment out of their lives
>To wander in the unknown lands
>Where life for the most part is like oil and water,
>Then they would've realized
>That they haven't even scratched the surface
>Of what they call life!
>People who strive to live their lives
>Like milk and water are not from my world.
>How could they be!
>When all their time on earth all they do
>Is obsessively ruminate on how to escape
>From their life's hardships at any cost;
>And find a way to live in comfort
>And constant pleasure,
>Where an abundance of milk and honey
>Is always up for grabs.
>When I wander through unknown lands,
>Some of the people that I encounter on my path
>Give me a dirty look.
>Their look is dirtier than I look!
>At times I'm filthy and unfailingly poor,
>I beg for food and money to survive;
>And in return from humbling myself,
>I receive the freedom from my pride
>And ego trip that causes my arrogance to arise;
>And for making such a small sacrifice
>My reward is rich awareness in all my surroundings

ZEK

In both internal and external realms.
People like me without a roof over their heads,
Without a crumb of bread on their plates,
Without a dime to their names,
Who aimlessly wander around the world
And encounter all kinds of folks on their paths;
Consequently put the essence of each
Encountered man's character to the test
When they see a vagabond in need of help.
From all the wonders that I've seen in both realms,
Till this very day,
I haven't seen anything better
Than a kind soul,
Who brings the light to a crippled soul
Who was consumed by darkness.
To show compassion is the greatest
Of all men's achievements;
And it is the sole reason why!
A mankind continues to thrive,
Instead of withering like a plant
During the dry seasons.
I have no need to find myself a home,
For the world is my home,
Nor do I dream of a place
That I would want to visit.
Instead, I roam the lands to all directions
Without a preexisting plan in mind;
And I never visit the same place twice,
No matter how beautiful and comfortable
It might appear to be to my eyes;
Since if I would've gotten attached
To one specific place,
Then the beauty in my mind would melt away
Just like the snow once the sun rises;
And I would become confined to my own mind
Like an owl to its own forest

Whose spirit was born to be free,
And yet, it is trapped willingly
Like it lives in a bird cage.
I keep my distance from all the wonderous places
That I once visited,
So I could keep myself in constant wonder
From where I might end up the next day.
The present moment is all I live for.
It is where the heart of my life is,
And I have no care for what tomorrow might bring;
And as for my past,
I don't even try to remember what I ate for breakfast
Never mind about trying to remember
My long-lived wandering life;
And it is because of this path
That I've managed to see the world
From all the angles.
I've seen the night sky
From the high mountains
Whose stars were within my hand's reach
That many cannot even fathom in their mind's eye,
How beautiful the world looks
From a home without a roof;
Unless they too will choose
To live their lives like a vagabond.
You can live the rest of your life
Like a small bird stuck on the twig
In the birdline,
Or like an owl who believes
That the forest that it dwells in
Is all there is to this world,
Or, like a vagabond
Who roams enthusiastically the unknown lands
To feed the heart of his soul
With wonderous life.

ZEK

I thanked the vagabond for his enlightening words, and as we both parted our own way without any further words, I looked up into the sky and saw the raven hovering below a clear cloud.

Day VI
The Middle Path

On the way back, I paced without haste as the words of the vagabond rang in my head, making me ponder deeper into my thoughts of how there was no right or wrong path, but simply a path; and what I do on that path is what will determine the outcome of *mayéyi zhízni* (my life). These thoughts led me to remember of the middle path that was *menti*oned to me by my *diadía* at the beginning of my retreat.

He said, "*V syó v zhízni* (Everything in life) has to be properly balanced, whether it's sleeping, eating, working, studying, or purifying your mind.

"When you don't reap the benefits from your hard work, then you need to reevaluate your *zhízn* (life) and try the middle path instead.

"By trying too hard or not enough, both actions will result in failures. When you over-indulge yourself in daily activities, over time it becomes harmful to your body and mind. Although over-working can bring temporary comfort to your life, in the long run it will increase the suffering as the mind will become frustrated and confused and exhaust the body from not understanding why it doesn't benefit from its hard work as it should; and when you don't try enough, you simply will come short every time from reaping the benefits of your half-work.

"Over-indulging comes from our insatiable desires to have comfort in life. It even applies to the Buddhist practice; for instance, the meditation practice which helps to purify the body and the mind, since when the meditation is practiced for too long it becomes counter-productive and even dangerous to our body and mind, just as everything else that we overdo. Even too much of good deeds will turn into *yád* (a poison), since when a person is constantly looking for a way to help others, he eventually becomes obsessed with it; and then his obsession to do good turns into *narkótik* (a drug), *narkótik* that he gets high off. He becomes addicted to good deeds, and when he doesn't get high, he begins to suffer internally.

"Therefore, *vsyó v zhízni* (everything in life) has to be properly balanced, since when one thing in life is unbalanced then everything else becomes off as well.

> "Buddha said,
> 'Desire is like salty water,
> The more you drink
> The thirstier you become.'
> The cravings overpower us
> It always wants and needs.
> As it feeds on our weaknesses
> Like a parasite that leeches onto us
> And drains us slowly out of our energy.
> And when dark days don't get any brighter
> And the path to persevere
> Doesn't come to fruition.
> Then instead of blaming everything
> And everyone around you, including yourself,
> Take the middle path,
> The path that leads to harmony.
> The more difficult the practice is,

The harder it is to stay on the right path,
And with less work,
It is easier to lose your way;
But by taking the middle path,
The practice becomes not too strenuous
Or too effortless,
But just right to reap the higher reward.
Continue on your path
And everything that you have lost
Will come back to you tenfold."

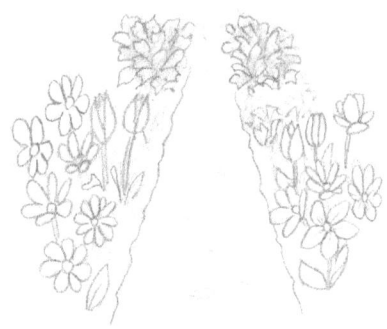

Day VI
That Place

As I came out of the forest and walked into the garden where I saw monks and practitioners practicing walking meditation, I joined them without hesitation, and on the next lap I was joined by my *díadía* (uncle). It was peaceful and very ruminating to be walking in silence with him, where silence was present not only externally, but internally in me as well.

The clouds gathered gradually over the monastery and the sky became engulfed by the arising darkness. Soon after that the lamps around the housing were being lit by the lamplighter who looked exactly like the same large *manáh* (monk) with a limp who on my first day guided me to my room. All of the monks and practitioners began to head in and get ready for supper, and then as usual, to end the night with the night's meditation and *dharma* talk with *roshi*.

My *díadía* and I stood silently under an orchard of a peach tree, but then the silence was interrupted by the night owl's hooting, and my *díadía* began to speak as if he had to get something off his chest.

"*Mayá zhízn* (My life) has been difficult, to the point that at times it was excruciatingly unbearable to deal with all the never-ending hardships. There were moments *v mayéyi zhízni* (in my life) when I felt that after surviving such difficulties I would be able to endure anything *v mayéyi zhízni* with ease. *No ya bil ne prav*! (But I was wrong!), since life's sufferings are easier to endure while residing in part of the realm where *zhízn* (life) has little or no value; since when I returned into the realm where *mayá dushá* (my spirit) was free to roam as it pleased, every little pebble that I stepped on felt like nails were going through my feet; and every little predicament that I encountered on my path was magnified by a hundred fold; and when I once again found myself in that place, where *zhízn* had little or no value, same or even worse situations that would arise throughout the day when I was in a place where *mayá dushá* was free to roam around as it pleased, then it wouldn't even cause me to lose my sleep over them; and it was in that place where I realized that it was that difficult life that changed me and gradually molded me to endure my life's hardships with much ease.

"*Ti znáyesh*! (You know!), when I went *v tyur'mú* (to prison) for the first time, it was before you were even born; and I was much, much younger when you ended up there yourself.

"When I was in that place
Every day I felt like I was going into the fray,
And dying was not what scared me,
But surviving in such a way
That would make me forget who I was
At the end of each day.
What kept me in touch with reality
Was to keep reminding myself where I came from,
Even if that place was filled with darkness,
Loneliness, and nothing but pain;
And where I once was one of those

ZEK

Who till this very day continue to perish
From never-ending bloody wars,
And never stop praying with tears in their eyes
Without any answers to their cries;
And just because I no longer reside
In that soul-wrecking place
I should never forget,
Nor feel ashamed of my own past;
Nor turn my back on all of those who sacrificed their lives,
So I could have a better life
That many only dream of having.
Regardless how gloomy my life once was
I still owe it to that dark place,
For it was because of that soul-draining place
That I was molded to the last wrinkle on my face
And became the person that I am nowadays."

Day VI
Nonviolent Way

It wasn't long after our *dharma* talk that we both headed to the dining hall for supper where we had a fish soup. As we sat and ate, a big guy who was bigger than me and my *diadía* (uncle) put together, the same *kashalót* (sperm whale) who ate all of the blueberry jam earlier this morning, went for seconds, and then thirds… until there was nothing left in the soup pot.

We ate without saying a word to each other, although we did glance at each other in acknowledgement. My thoughts drifted and I visualized myself being back *v tyur'mé* (in prison), in a chow hall, sitting and eating, and every *manáh* (monk) and practitioner were dressed in the prison scrubs. My *diadía* who sat across from me was eating his soup calmly as he always does, breaking bread with his fingers and soaking it into the soup bowl, and then putting it into his mouth. His tattooed fingers on his left hand read "*BOG*" ("GOD"), and on his other hand "*ZEK*" ("convict/Prisoner").

As much as I love my uncle, I'm glad that we were never together *v tyur'mé*, since I heard crazy stories about him when he did his time back in *Sibíri* (Siberia) in the Gulag prison. Everyone was afraid of him, even *mentí* (guards). He was notoriously known for stabbing other *zékav* (convicts) who crossed him. He would stab first, then ask questions later to resolve the issue, that is if the guy would still be around to talk after my *diadía* was finished with him.

His reputation amongst *bratvá* (brotherhood) for making people pay in a violent way when they double-crossed him pursued him to the U.S. even years after he had left *S.S.S.R.* (U.S.S.R.). I'm glad he changed and found his way with the Buddhism, since I would hate to be around my old *diadía* to whom I would have to always prove that I don't take *gavnó* (shit) from anybody.

Yá pónil (I understood) long before I came to *tyur'mú* (prison) that violence was not the way to resolve problems. I guess that was why I chose *zhízn vará* (life of a thief) and not of a violent criminal. Many of my *bratvá* (brotherhood) carried guns and knives with them at all times. I, on the other hand, never developed such obsession for weapons, although I did have *kastét* (a knuckle-duster) with me so in case I did get into a fight I would knock a guy out with one punch, instead of like my *bratvá* who would pull their guns and knives out and try to kill a poor fellow who regretfully would cross his path with them. I always believed that if I were to carry a weapon with me, then eventually I would use it, and that could end very badly for both of us. There would be no winners. It happened to one of my friends who pulled a knife out on a guy in a club when he got into a scuffle with him and was stabbed in the heart with his own knife. He died instantly, and the guy who killed him went to prison for many years. In the end, both lives were ruined because the weapon was involved in an argument that could've been resolved in a nonviolent way.

V tyur'mé (In prison) for many *zékav* (cons) the violence never subsided. If anything, it even escalated. Violence was always the first solution to their problems. For the most part, when *zéki* (convicts) acted with violence it was against each other and it was to demonstrate to the rest how brave and dangerous they were. In other words, it was to instill fear upon others, when in fact most were terrified themselves from living *v tyur'mé* where most *zéki* would not think twice to use *nozh* (a knife) against each other. This lifestyle was no different from the one most *zéki* led outside the prison walls. It's like they were stuck in their old ways, scared to change and try a different approach, a nonviolent way. In both cases, resolving their arising problems in a nonviolent way was foreign to them. It was something that was never tried before, and the fear of the unknown was what prevented many to take that first step, since what if it didn't work? Then their reputation could be ruined, and they would be seen in the eyes of other *zékav* as being weak, and that will make other cons take advantage of them all because they decided to take a nonviolent way and not to retaliate against other convicts who crossed them or disrespected them. *Tyur'má* (Prison) is not the right place to be practicing compassion, since *v tyur'mé* everyone is *volk* (a wolf). Even a sheep eventually grows claws and fangs. Not understanding that *tyur'má* is a ruthless place can severely cause *zek* (a prisoner) physical and emotional harm. That is why many *zéki* would rather be feared than loved, and seek revenge, even if one has to dig two graves, one for the victim and another for oneself.

However, the fact remained that *zéki* who looked to resolve conflicts with violence first would always find themselves in constant turmoil during their time *v tyur'mé*. They were always fighting either with *mentámi* (guards), the rival gangs, and/or with convicts from other neighborhoods, and even amongst their own *bratvá*. Over time such a negative way of life became the norm for them. It became part of their lives as if the act of violence was engraved into their minds like they were genetically molded with the purpose to act in a violent way without even realizing that there existed other options, the nonviolent ways, to resolve their problems. One thing that many ignored was that regardless of how strong they were physically or even mentally, they were still human beings with a mind that is fragile; since after causing harm to others to resolve their issues, it still takes a toll on the person's mind. The negative actions gradually begin to affect all human beings internally to the point that the pain and suffering increases when it is ignored by them.

ZEK

For me, over time it just became tiresome, too painful for my own internal growth. I no longer desired to take part in trying to fight with other *zékami* (convicts) over every little thing just because it was the way how *zéki* must act within *bratvá*; and if someone were to challenge their way, then he is looked upon as a traitor, a weak *zek* who doesn't deserve to be one of them. I ended up being one of those *zékav* who challenged the entire process of how *bratvá* should act *v tyur'mé* (in prison) by introducing a nonviolent way to resolve problems. When I proposed that in the future we should try to talk with a *zek* with whom we have a problem instead of fighting him, I was laughed at; and when they realized that I wasn't joking, they thought that *yá paterial rázum* (I lost my mind). Some *zéki* whom I knew for years and was good friends with stopped talking to me altogether. They said that if don't follow the rules of *bratvá*, then I should not be part of them.

And when one day my name came up to fight another guy as a retaliation who happened to be a friend of mine from a rival gang, I had to make my point. I, instead of resolving a problem in a violent way as I had done so in the past, squashed the whole issue with a simple good conversation. However, when *pahán bratví* (the boss of the brotherhood) heard about what I'd done, I was not only hated for it, but also got kicked out from my *bratvá*, after taking a beating, of course; and if I wasn't my uncle's nephew, I could've been easily killed for breaking the rules.

Being out of *bratvá* was the best thing that had happened to me *v tyur'mé*. The way I looked at it, it was a small price to pay with a few bruises, since I felt free from being constantly engaged *v tyurémskayi palítiki* (in prison politics) which was nothing but gossiping, arguing, fighting, and selling drugs. And once my headache was finally gone, I could see much clearer; and look at all of the *zékav* who took part in this vicious cycle of perpetual ignorance, and say to myself, I cannot believe that I used to be that *zek* who took orders from *kretína* (an idiot) like some kind of *sabáka* (a dog).

But what gave me the drive to change my ways and seek a nonviolent path was when I saw myself who I was as a man. A person who did nothing but vile acts throughout most of his life. This path for me began *v di'ryé* (in a hole/segregation block) where I was isolated for the entire two months after a violent fight with another *zek* where we both were left with plenty of scars on our bodies. It occurred to me there that violence has always been part of my life; and that it arose from anger.

Buddha once said, "Anger is like picking up hot coals with bare hands and throwing them at a person that was hated;" and in the end both men get hurt, and instead of causing harm, wishing good to all of those who bring the anger out of us, and that is the best way to eradicate the anger and develop compassion.

"Are you ready to go to the *zendo*?" my *diadía* asked, interrupting my thoughts in the process.

"*Da!* (Yeah!)" I said while holding on to my ruminating thoughts. We both got up and followed a group exiting the dining hall and then headed to the meditation hall.

I sat next to my *diadía* on the *zaffu*, and next to me sat *kashalót* (sperm whale). Me and my *diadía* were sitting in a half lotus and meditating as we awaited the *roshi's* arrival while *kashalót* had placed two more *zaffus* under his butt and had his knees raised up like he was sitting on a small toilet. My mind desperately itched to have a piece of calm tonight and be fully aware of my meditation, but *kashalóta* (the sperm whale's) heavy breathing was like hearing a horse breathe, which disturbed my mindfulness, and I instead of meditating went on pondering on my thoughts.

V di'ryé (In a hole) many *zéki* loved to make noise. It was as if silence was their worst enemy, while noise made them feel safer in some way, like it protected them from not only other *zékav* (convicts) but also from their internal selves.

At first, I tried to make as much noise as I possibly could to block that part of me that was trying to arise. I sang and even danced, but mostly listened to my Walkman; until the batteries died and I lost my voice from singing too loud; and then the silence that I was so afraid of began to rise within me; and I had no other option but to give in and face myself and see myself for who I had become and the man that dwelled within. I didn't see it back then how everything that I needed to achieve to free myself from the pain and suffering that tormented me was already within me. All I needed to do to realize that was to be in silence.

"When a man is completely alone
It is hard to make noise for him,
And that is when the silence creeps up

> And engulfs the mind with calm and peace
> Like the night consumes the sky;
> And that is when the most hidden,
> Shameful moments start to arise,
> Along with delusions that torment the mind,
> And in the process triggers within the self,
> To face yourself, and see yourself
> For who you truly are as a man."

And as far as I'm concerned, no man full of sins and shame ever wants to look within his heart and face himself. I know I didn't for as long as I could, since it takes courage, a real genuine person to look into one's own *sérdze* (heart) and admit to oneself that it is rotten; and accept one's wicked acts for being nothing more than vile. This is not an easy part to fulfill, and for this reason alone not many men muster to bring themselves to choose to live their lives in a nonviolent way.

Roshi entered into the *zendo* and a bolt of energy rushed through my body. I felt relieved as my thoughts dispersed like an insignificant cloud, and I found myself conscious of the present moment.

Day VI
True Practice

"*Buddha* once said," *roshi* said, "'Everything in the world arises, changes and perishes; nothing remains constant for even a single moment,' and although we all know this in our hearts, yet some ignore this fact as if it is not true. Those who evade the facts of life for what they are, lead their lives in a blissful ignorance; and finding their path to enlightenment makes their journey from difficult to impossible.

"Ignorance can be something that is not knowing, or it can also be the perverted knowledge, thinking that what you know is true when in fact it is not; and it can also be living in denial, such as refusing to accept the truth because it is not what you want to hear.

"Unfortunately, the more ignorant a person is, the more often he will endure the hardships and his path will seem nearly impossible to complete, while the more enlightened a person becomes, the more prosperous his life will be, and the path that he is on will appear easier and more enjoyable to be on.

"Ultimately, our karmic actions are driven by our understanding of life, and by reflecting on the sufferings and prosperities of both the ignorant and the enlightened individuals can further cultivate understanding of our practice.

"Overall, life is never easy for either man. Even for an enlightened person it is still challenging, since an open-minded person always has to make self-sacrifices to further expand his mind.

"Once an enlightened person becomes aware of his *Buddha-nature*, the ability to combine his attained wisdom and compassion and put it to practice, he has to work even harder to maintain it, since the mind is like water, if it stagnates for too long then it turns into a swamp.

"Therefore, the practice to eradicate ignorance and grow understanding never ends. It is a lifetime, dedicated practice that you all have briefly experienced so far throughout the *sesshin*.

"The true practice is not only carried out physically and verbally, but also within the mind. You all must control your mind to the point that it will start to generate positivity and avoid giving rise to the negative thoughts. Taming the mind will improve discipline and understanding toward developing the inner peace. If you have inner peace, then the external problems do not affect your mind, since in life there is only one kind of peace which dwells internally; and it can only be attained by a disciplined mind that can generate a long-lasting happiness, and not as much as physical actions, such as prostrating, bowing; or verbal actions, such as reciting mantras, chanting, and positive speech; since all of that can be practiced while the mind continues to harbor ill will."

Day VI
Two Waters

During meditation I felt as if I was not one with myself. I don't know what it exactly was, the salty fish soup or feeling sorry for myself for not practicing as I should according to *roshi*; but I felt as if all my life I was drinking salty water, and the more I drank, the more my desires insatiably grew stronger; and then, I would find myself in a place where I often wished I didn't end up. I'm talking about the place where my mind takes me when it craves more from *zhízni* (life).

> "I feel like all of my life I've lived
> In two different realms.
> In one like milk and water
> And in the other like oil and water;

ZEK

And I can honestly say,
A man who lives a life like milk and water
Is truly free and alive,
While a man who lives a life like oil and water
Is trapped,
And just as good as lying dead—
Dead in a grave.
A man who is free has access to both
External and internal realms
Where his spirit can attain a perfect balance
From living a fulfilling life
In both realms.
While a man who is trapped has only access
To the internal realm
Where his spirit is always dissatisfied
From living an unbalanced life
In the realm he wishes he would've never dwelled.
Thus, a man who lives an unbalanced life
Can never fully develop his soul,
Until his heart has been fully satisfied
From living to the fullest
In both realms.
A man who lives a life like milk and water
Always has a voice,
He is heard in both realms;
While a man who lives a life like oil and water
Can cry all he wants
And no one will ever hear his voice
In the external realm.
No wonder when a trapped man's cry
Has been ignored for a lingering period of time,
His soul fills with so much anger
From bitterness and pain in life
That his moral judgment to distinguish
Between what is good and wicked
Becomes fractured;

And since it is easier to be more noticed
When one does evil instead of good;
Thus, he often does
What he thinks could be the only way
To show his existence to the external realm,
Even if it means at the cost
Of poisoning his own heart,
And causing grave evil upon others.
When a trapped man ruminates infinitely
On nothing else but how to escape
From an unwanted realm,
He then misses the entire existence
Of the fruitful life that dwells within
The internal realm.
When a free man believes with all his conviction
That a trapped man does not deserve to live his life
Like milk and water.
He then insinuates without saying,
That a trapped man does not deserve to exist
In either of the two realms.
But I say,
There should only be one type of man
Who should live his life like oil and water,
And that is a man
Who is lying dead—
Dead in a grave."

Day VI
Betrayal

I laid in bed and gradually was falling asleep; and as I gazed at the lit candle that was flickering high and low from a light breeze coming through an open window above my head, a thought arose, and I thought to myself, here we go again! For every time my mind rests, it begins to ruminate and take me far away; and in the end, leaving me alone engulfed in my own ruminating thoughts.

It was never easy, I thought to myself, to be a good guy. To remain good takes a great amount of work, and the more I worked on myself, the more *yá pónil* (I understood) how easy life would've been for me if I was *dermóvin chelavékam* (a shit-bag).

I had a chance to avoid my prison sentence altogether when the two F.B.I. agents came to see me at the beginning of my prison bid and offered to release me for a price to work for them against the Russian organized crime. I could've avoided all my hardships by saying *da!* (yes!) to them, but then what kind of a man would I be then? Nothing more than a fake for the rest of my life. *Mayá dusha yi móyi duh* (My soul and my spirit) were not forged this way, and there must be a reason why they both chose to make me live my life in such a difficult way. In truth, if I would've gone against the nature of my soul and spirit, then they would've left my body and I would've been *pustyím chelavékam* (an empty man), a walking corpse and nothing more.

And so, when I said these words to them, their faces looked as if they were about to poop, for one of the F.B.I. agents said, "You are one of the few who said no to us. The majority of the *bratvá* don't let a chance like that slip through their fingers."

"Well, I'm not like most! It's not in my heart nor in my nature to be a treacherous man," I said and left the room.

Da! (Yes!) the path that I chose was difficult and even unbearable at times to endure that prison *zhízn* (life); but in the end the preservation of *mayéyi dushí yi dúha* (my soul and spirit) was what was at stake. And it all was worth it, since I can proudly say to myself that I have survived and didn't crumble, although it did leave me damaged in a way. And I guess it explains the reason why the damaged ones, the ones who lived and suffered without light at the end of their tunnel, are more *prasveshyóníyi* (enlightened) than those who never were devoured by the total *tyemnatóyi* (darkness).

The damaged ones who have experienced *zhízn* in the dark and light; who found themselves abandoned and alone, know the true value of *zhízni* (life) and what it means to fight to its last to preserve the essence of one's being. The easiest way known to man is to live a life only for oneself and no one else; and do what is best only for oneself even if it means in the process to bring other men misery, despair, and destruction. To betray another *chelavéka* (man) is the lowest that a man can ever do to his own *dushé yi dúhu* (soul and spirit).

You know how they say, "Keep your friends close, but your enemies closer?" Well, all of that changed the day when *móyi lútshíyi droog* (my best friend) whom I used to call *moyim bratam* (my brother) betrayed me. After that my entire philosophy and ideology of what *bratvá* stood for was going down the drain. I lost all respect for anyone whom I once called *moyím droógam yi brátam* (my friend and brother). I cut all contact with all of them and wanted nothing to do with any of them, since what is *droog íli brät* (friend or brother) anyway? A person whom you are supposed to trust! But then, seriously! For how long? I believe that the worst thing that any man can do is to believe that he has *droog* (a friend) whom he can trust.

If there is a person who knows every little dirt that you have done. Who knows what truly dwells inside *tvayóm sérdze* (your heart). Who knows what makes you laugh, cry, and bleed. Then the question is not if, but when, he will turn on you; and then, how are you going to defend yourself against such a powerful enemy? I know I couldn't. This *súkin sín* (son of a bitch) knew more about me than *Bog* (God) himself, and he used it for his own advantage to get himself a sweeter deal.

I always believed that *móyi droog, móyi brät* (my friend, my brother) had my back, and what I mean by that is that he would back me up and not put *nózh* (a knife) in it. Till this day I still feel the dagger lodged in my back, and I still cannot believe that he sold me down the river to *mentám* (the cops) to save his own neck from going *v tyur'mú* (to prison) for the crime that he himself had committed; and to weasel himself out of the prison he told *mentám* (the cops) that it was I who stole the box of jewelry; and a few days after the robbery the cops quietly waited for me in the house of my room where the box of jewelry was hidden. I knew right from the first moment I saw *mentóv* (cops) in the room, for he was the only person who I'd told where I hid the box. What a rookie mistake that was on my part. I guess what I didn't see was how envious of me he was becoming seeing me prosper when he was not. Shame that was on my part, for I couldn't see it in his eyes the hatred that was seething out of his pores. His *pridátel'stva* (betrayal) not only sent me to the slammer for 20 years, but it made me lose all hope in all mankind to ever have a lick of trust in them for many years to come. Even nowadays, I still have great doubts if I should ever open myself to another person.

You know the proverb that I mentioned earlier? Well, I changed it into my own words of virtue, which now says, "Keep your enemies close, but your friends closer," since what I learned that day was how *pridátel'stva* happens mostly by the people who you least expect it from and who happen to be closest to us. Overall, this *pridátel'stva* had hindered my positive growth to the point that it made me paranoid of other people who were trying to get to know me; and without trust, relationships could not be built. Because of that I've lost many opportunities in my life to learn from other people. For a long time, I refused to believe that amongst traitors and manipulators there were also loyal and honest people who genuinely wanted to help when they saw me in despair. During those hurtful years, I wouldn't turn to people for help even if *mayá zhízn* (my life) depended on it, no matter how desperately I struggled to gain some insight on my gloomy life.

My strong craving for knowledge and wisdom, and my desire to heal from pain, led me to turn to writing poetry. As whack as it may sound, writing about love, despair, loss, and internal and spiritual struggles was what kept me intact as a human being throughout my time *v tyur'mé* (in prison). Poetry opened my heart and made me understand myself better as a man and who I'm aiming to become; and it brought me out of my loathing for my "friend" who so shamelessly *pridál minyá* (betrayed me). Although, it did not make me forgive him or any person in that case who caused me harm, but it did bring me a peace of mind for as long as I continued to write; but most importantly, it brought to a stop the hypocrisy within me. Who was I to loathe someone else for his wickedness when I myself have done so many wrongs?

I had an opportunity to get my revenge for what *móyi droog* (my friend) did to me; but I just couldn't bring myself to cause him harm. Perhaps if I'd had a chance to get my revenge on him before he testified in court against me to get a deal for the crime that he committed and got caught for, then I would've done it without a second thought; but as years passed and I understood life more, I simply let it all go. I guess I just got tired of holding on to my revenge and a feeling of constant loathing, because when I let it go, I started to trust people a little more, and I just didn't want to go backwards with my progress and lose all of that which took me so long to finally attain.

> One lesson I learned from all of this
> Was to never hate the man
> Who so shamelessly betrayed me in the end;
> For all he did was to reveal

ZEK

The true essence of his soul to me.
He was always that treacherous man
Who was conniving behind my back
In his own twisted mind.
The hatred that I felt for him,
In truth was not for him but for myself;
For it was I who failed so ignorantly to see
That treacherous soul
That dwelled within him all along,
When so many signs were displayed
Quite vividly in front of me,
Yet, I chose out of my own ignorance
To look the other way,
And for that I paid dearly
With my own life.

Day VI
The Key

I finally fell asleep, I think, or was I just thinking in my sleep? Not sure I knew the answer, but in either case, I saw myself being back in the place that I wouldn't come back to even at gunpoint, although this time it was not like *tyur'má* (the prison). Not exactly! But instead, a zoo, which on second thought wasn't much of a difference, and instead of animals trapped in *klétkah* (cages) there were people, and I was amongst them in my own private *klétki* (cage); and that wasn't even the craziest part about it. The insane part about my dream was how the animals were free, walking around like people who come to the zoo to see their fa*vo*red *zveryéyi* (animals).

All kinds of animals stopped by at my *klétki*, admiring me for the beautiful specimen that I was, but none of them liked me enough to see me out of my cage free. Some even checked the gate of the cage to make sure that it was properly secured tight in its place, since in their eyes, I was still *díkiyi zvér* (a wild beast) who could attack them violently if I was to be released.

Truthfully, seeing animals walking freely at the zoo like people and pointing their fingers at my *klétku* (cage) made me realize that that is what I would've done to them if I too was free like them, and if I was, I too would've been pointing my finger at the animals that I have never seen nor understood, and I would've been terrified of these *díkih zveryéyi* (wild beasts) if they were to be released.

I can honestly say that *mayá zhízn* (my life) that I once considered to be the bottom of the cesspool was in fact not so; since there is no limit to how low life can get. There is always worse after being worse, just as it is with better. And the things that terrified me the most in the past no longer do now in the present, for I have experienced both sides of life, one within *klétki* (the cage) and the other from outside; and what I have learned throughout my life was that it all comes down to the life experience in the end. To fully understand the things that I grappled with my entire life were not the words that I read and listened to; but the way I applied all that I learned to my life, and that is what truly made my life more meaningful.

This *klétka* (cage) that I found myself trapped in, at times it was a healthy place, a place of calm and prayer, meditation, and *prasveshéniya* (enlightenment) where I was feeling proud of the man that I was becoming; but then, at other times it was a place of pure despair, regrets and misery, and pure emptiness in my *sérdze* (heart) where I felt ashamed of who I was becoming.

Throughout my *zhízn* (life) I've been molded by misfortunes and unexpected hardships to become someone whose nature was not mine. And now, I'm remolding myself into *chelavéka* (a man) who I was destined to become. Everything that I ever wanted I once already had, but just couldn't see what I had until it all was gone; and now I'm just fighting to get it all back by applying all the lessons that I've learned throughout my lonely path.

For the first time in my life, I became grateful for *zhízn* (the life) that I once had; and it was during the time of complete loss of hope from ever seeing light when my rigid mind began to unlock. I felt light illuminating from within me, when for a long time it was dimmed by gloom and doom that kept me *v temnatyé* (in the dark), preventing me from seeing my path that was now in front of me.

> I guess I could blame the darkness that dwelled within me
> For keeping me away from the light that was all along within me.
> The darkness made me want to run and hide.
> But I didn't run nor did I hide;
> Instead, for some unknown reason
> I dug and dug relentlessly deep into the heart of my heart,
> I went to places that I would've never even dared to visit
> In my lifetime with a single thought;
> For all it ever did was to bring a revolting feeling in my gut,
> From being dissatisfied each time with what I had found
> In my heart.
> I faced my worst enemy, myself!
> And searched and searched, as I had said, relentlessly,
> For what my hungry soul has been craving for all along.

A feeling of bliss aroused within me while I was asleep, or was I just thinking in my sleep? As if I had discovered the hidden key to the cage's gate that kept me trapped inside from living a life that I was desperately craving. The key that I had found was inside of me all along; and yet, I searched for it for so long in the most dark, unknown places known to my heart without any luck since I could last remember. The key that I held was inside my mind. It had no form. No weight. No sound. No color. No smell. No taste. Instead, it had many, many different words all scrambled in my mind, and all I had to do was to put them in the proper order. All I had to do was to write *poému* (a poem) and whisper it into the lock hanging on the gate. How hard could that be, I thought!

I think I woke up in the middle of the night from the cold chill and not from the eerie dream. The candle on the bureau was still lit, flickering as it tried to stay *zhivóyi* (alive) by keeping the flame from dimming out, but the stick of wax of the candle was almost burned to the bottom of the plate. I closed the window and blew out the candle, or did I do all of that in my sleep? But the last thing that I remember was how I was whispering the key words into the lock hanging on the gate of *klétki* (the cage) that kept me trapped inside.

> How can I say,
> That I am different than other men.
> When I was created out of the same
> Elements as all men.
> To claim otherwise
> Would be nothing but a lie;
> But the only difference remains
> Between them and I
> That I can say is true,
> Is what I had gathered in my soul
> Throughout my life;
> And that is something that every man
> Would agree and say,
> That they are not the same like other men.
> I wish I could say,
> That my soul is pure;
> But that would be a lie.
> It is just as full of sins
> That every man is guilty of,
> And so am I;
> I am different from other men
> When I say,
> That the only difference remains
> Between them and I,
> Is that I am not ashamed to admit
> All the wicked deeds that I had gathered in my soul
> Throughout my life;
> And that is something that every man
> Would agree and say,
> That they are not the same like other men.
> There is not a single soul
> That is exactly alike,
> Just like the sins that we all had gathered in our souls
> Throughout our lives;

But one part that does make me feel unique,
Is when I say,
That I am no different than other men…
Except for my soul and sins.

Day VII
Zen

The door opened wide in my room, and my *díadía* (uncle) was standing inside calling my name. It took me a minute or two to wake up and then just as much to understand what he was saying; and as I was beginning to arise on my feet, I started to hear his voice loud and clear.

"You are late for meditation! You have already missed breakfast and *dharma* talk! Get up! Get dressed! I will be waiting for you in the *zendo*."

I couldn't believe that I slept through the sounds of the gong. *Bliad!* (Shit!) I really was hoping to get some breakfast. I miss that crunchy cheese pizza at the Bon-Jorno that Chef Fat-Tony makes. I miss my job as the janitor/dishwasher for I do work with good people who are kind and understanding of what I went through. Chef Fat-Tony, who is also the owner of *restarána* (the restaurant), always asks me if I need anything. He always, at the end of my shift, puts in the bag leftovers for me to take back with me home. And if I'm not mistaken, I still have a slice or two of cheese pizza left in my fridge that I would love to get my hands on right about now. I'm so hungry that I could eat like that *kashalót* (sperm whale) who ate all the fish soup last night. Hmmm… fish soup!

On the way to the *zendo* my stomach churned, telling me "*Nakarmí menyá!* (Feed me!)" I still couldn't believe that I missed breakfast. It was like I fell under a spell, a strong desire to rest.

This practice takes a toll on my mind and body. It is most definitely not easy! I've endured extremely difficult hardships in life, and I tell you what, this practice is most definitely one of the hardest ones I've ever done. As hungry as I am now, there were moments *v mayéyi zhízni* (in my life) when I haven't eaten for days. Ever since I've been out of prison, I've become soft. After making myself comfortable for living an uncomfortable life for 20 years, and now forcing myself to go back to the old ways that I thought that I would never have to relive ever again; however, that is the fact, and that is something that I've learned throughout the week, is that being uncomfortable is part of life. *Zhízn* (life) is full of uncomfortable surprises. It is like one day you could have everything in life you ever dreamed of, but then the next you are dying of thirst and there is not a single soul that can come and help you. So, *vozmí sibyá v rúki* (get yourself together), I said to myself and entered into the *zendo* right as they were about to start to meditate. I saw my *díadía* sitting in the back row. I went and sat by his side.

"*Dóbraye útra!* (Good morning!) he said.

"*Dóbraye!* (Morning!) I said.

I was 30 minutes into my meditation when I found myself completely free of all distractions. Not a single thought aroused. My mind was entirely under my control in a state of inner serenity, fully absorbed in pure concentration. I entered into *samadhi*, a state of total meditation in which my mind rested without wavering as it became one with oneself.

Roshi whacked the *jukpi* on his palm, and my pure concentration was no longer pure.

"How do we think of not thinking?

"Non-thinking is what we are trying to achieve. Not letting your mind rest anywhere in a moment. If it rests without concentration, then our thoughts arise and take control of our mind. Non-thinking is the *Zen* practice!

"In *Zen*, it is a pure act that matters. An act that can only be done wholeheartedly. A mind is nothing but fantasies and regrets, which causes us to get caught up in the past and the future, neglecting us to stay awake in the present where it can be full of life.

"With *Zen* practice your goal becomes to see yourself for who you are, here and now in this present moment.

"Don't ever be afraid to see yourselves for who you are! Let go of your past, your regrets, and arising fantasies. Tame your wandering mind through breathing and stay awake.

"To wake up literally means to awaken from our fantasies, to enter into a life of the present moment of clarity; and to find yourself in a moment of silence, peacefulness, and non-agitation."

Roshi's voice had dissipated into thin air like he never even spoke, and we all resumed back to our meditation. I couldn't help myself but to think of this one incident when I was back *v tyur'mé* (in prison).

I remember when I was in a lockdown unit for a fight where I stayed for six months straight as a punishment, and there was this *ment* (guard) by the name of Sheet-Bag. It was a name that *zéki* (convicts) gave him, since every time he would come into the unit he would begin to yell at *zékav* (prisoners) demanding that *zéki* remove their sheets off their iron-barred doors that they used to block the view from the outside into their cells. Every time when Sheet-Bag would come into our unit, there would always be some *zek* who would yell out to give the rest of the cons a heads up.

"Sheet-Bag! He is back!" *zek* would yell.

And then the rest of us would join in and begin to yell all together. "Hey, look everyone! It is Sheet-Bag! He is back!"

This would go on for as long as it took until he would get pissed off and storm out of the unit.

I don't know why I remembered this particular story. Perhaps remembering it would always cheer me up, and because no matter how bad *zhízn v tyur'mé* (life in prison) was for *zékav*, we all tried to laugh even in the darkest places. Otherwise, if life in such a place is taken too seriously, it would swallow even the toughest *zékav zhivími* (prisoners alive).

> While being in the lockdown unit, I told myself,
> Who ever said that you have a right to be happy!
> This sense of having has been instilled in you
> Since your early years,
> By those who cared for you.
> But what they failed to tell you was,
> That this sense of a right to be happy in life
> It is not given, it is earned
> From overcoming the never-ending hardships in your life.
> This key ingredient to strive to be happy
> Was left out;
> And this is why you are disheartened with life
> When you don't feel happy.
> And now, I understand that life is suffering!
> And happiness, it comes and goes
> Depending on my karmic actions.

DAY VII
A FALLEN FRUIT

During lunch I put a real *kashalót* (sperm whale) to shame. My *diadía* (uncle) couldn't believe his eyes when I went for seconds and even thirds. I was competing with the *kashalót* for baked potatoes with fish and the salad. But I didn't care, I was starving. Ever since I started *sesshin* I must've lost 10 pounds.

"You definitely made up for the missed breakfast!" my uncle said.

"Hmmm…" I hummed in agreement with a full mouth, looking at the *kashalót* behind my *diadía* who was staring at me back with his hungry, angry eyes for taking the last piece of baked fish off the buffet plate. Usually during the retreat practitioners were not supposed to eat a lot. But that is easy for *manáhov* (the monks) to do who have practiced fasting for years, but for the new practitioners, particularly for the *kashalót* who was at least an easy 300 pounds, it was most definitely a challenge to eat three small meals a day.

After lunch my *diadia* and I walked to the back of the monastery where he does gardening. There were several greenhouses with seedlings that were already sprouting from the small cups, ready to be replanted into the soil.

He picked a fallen fruit from under a tree and took a bite, then spit it out instantly.

"Oooh! It is rotten to the core," he said with a sour face.

He then picked one from the tree and bit into it.

"Oooh! This one is even worse. I would've offered you one but it's at your own expense. However, you never know for sure what you will taste unless you try it for yourself," he said and threw a rotten apple in the compost pile next to the greenhouse.

"Just like it is with people! You can never know for sure who is who unless you put them through a test to see the true nature of their *dush* (souls) that dwell within them," I said.

"*Ti prav!* (You are right!) People and the fruits have more in common than we might think!"

He picked another fallen fruit off the ground, wiped it on the sleeve of his robe, and bit into it.

"Hmmm...*vkusniatina!* (Delicious!) Have you ever thought that:

> A fallen fruit has experienced more life
> Than the ones that are still clinching
> To a stem of a tree.
> For a fruit that has been shaken off violently of a tree
> By an angry wind, rolled around in dirt, mud,
> And laid in the puddle,
> Attacked and eaten by the insects, birds, and other animals,
> Scorched by the rays of the sun,
> And chilled by the cold of the night,
> Had experienced a true meaning of life
> By all of these pains and sufferings.
> And it is no different with all mankind
> Who have lived their lives just like the fallen fruits,

ZEK

And who were found to be just as pure or wicked to the core
As any other fallen fruit laying on the ground
And just like there is no certain way
To know for sure
Which one of the fruits is more rotten to the core,
So is the same with all…
That men encounter face to face
Without knowing for sure
What kind of a soul dwells within a man's core.
Unless of course one takes a chance
And picks a fallen fruit
That had been muddied, eaten, scorched, chilled, bruised
From the bottom of a tree,
Or the one that still clinches so innocently
To the stem of a tree,
And examines it in one's own bare hands as he takes a bite
To see whether it is fresh or rotten to the core.
And just as one would not continue
To indulge oneself in eating a rotten fruit,
So then one should not remain staying close to a man
Whose soul one finds being so disturbingly
Rotten to the core;
Unless of course one's soul is just as rotten.

DAY VII
THE WAYS OF OUR ANCESTORS

I stood on the edge of the precipice behind the monastery, looking into the horizon far beyond what my ordinary eyes could see. The mountain of trees below me and the ocean of sky above me were illuminated by the midday light of the sunrise. And deep inside the forest, I saw a hidden *izbú* (log cabin) with a thin smoke coming out from its chimney, spiraling up into the cloud *v nyebisá* (in the sky). And by the cabin's side, a sequoia tree. A tree that is born of fire; for after it rises, it falls… so it could rise out of its ashes even higher.

My curiosity overwhelmed me. It consumed my untamed mind to go see who dwelled in that *vstáriyi izbyé* (old log cabin). I walked down the mountain's narrow path that led me straight to the colossal tree and other trees that hid *izbú* (the log cabin) with its leafy branches.

"Hello!" I said, but there was no answer. I knocked on the front door, but there was no one inside. I walked to the back of the cabin and there I saw *starúshku* (a little old lady) feeding her hens and ducks. She had a shaved head and was dressed in the monk's robe. She looked like a Buddhist nun to me.

She saw me walking and said, "*Namaste!*" as she approached me.

"*Namaste!*" I said and bowed. "I saw your cabin from the top of the mountain and couldn't resist coming down to see who the dweller was of this beautiful log cabin. I would've never guessed that it would be a little old lady."

"Why is that?" she asked with a curiosity in her eyes, although her eyes also revealed that they already knew the answer to my response.

"Well, perhaps I'm not used to seeing an old woman living alone in a secluded place like a forest," I said, feeling that I answered correctly to justify my question.

"I guess you are right! You won't see many elderly women living alone in this part of the world, and particularly alone in the forest. But that is because folks have forgotten the ways of our ancestors; and that women are just like men. We experience the pains and sufferings from life and look for a way to find peace even if it means living in secluded places," she said.

"Oh! That part I know from my own personal experience that women are not that different from men when it comes to pains and sufferings." As I said this, I instantly thought of my *mátushka* (mother) who I saw in a lot of pain and suffering and desperately searching for a way out of it.

"You look like a new practitioner from the retreat?" she asked.

"Yes, I am! And today is the last day of the retreat," I responded with a sigh, like I have climbed to the top of the sequoia tree that stood like a mountain by the cabin.

"Oh! That is great! Have you learned a lot?" she asked.

"Too much and at the same time not enough, although I wish I had more time to stay longer and learn, for I feel like I haven't even scratched the surface of the practice," I said.

"Well, I tell you what! No matter how much you learn there will always be room to learn more, since for as long as you have a drive in your heart to continue on learning, you will always be searching, and in the process evolving no matter where you are. And that is something that has always been part of human nature, which is to have a drive in our hearts to expand our minds. And that has always been the ways of our ancestors," she said.

"What is the way of our ancestors?" I asked curiously.

"Well, let me tell you a story so you can understand it better," she said and paused for a moment to gather her thoughts.

"Long time ago there was a sage who sought to change the world. He understood that the pains and sufferings of the ordinary life turned folks' hearts into stone; and in order to change the world, first folks must change their own ways. They must go back to the ways of our ancestors; and so, the sage tried to touch folks' hearts with the teachings of our ancestors and promises to free them from the endless pains and sufferings of life; and if only folks would adapt the ways of our ancestors back into their lives and practice diligently with open minds, then the stone in their hearts will be removed and their hearts would begin to change, and with it the world.

"The sage's teachings were nothing more than just a reminder to the folks of what they had forgotten. And so, the sage reminded them of the ways of our ancestors:

"Folks who do not break bread with less fortunate ones
Have forgotten how to share good omen,
They have forgotten the ways of our ancestors.
Folks who do not greet one another when they meet on the path
Have forgotten how to love and respect each other,
They have forgotten the ways of our ancestors.
Folks who do not look each other in the eyes while conversing
Have forgotten that there is a living spirit inside of us all,
They have forgotten the ways of our ancestors.
Folks who do not forgive each other for their sins
Have forgotten how to be compassionate and understanding,
They have forgotten the ways of our ancestors.
Folks who do not take care of our Mother Earth
Have forgotten our Creator,
They have forgotten the ways of our ancestors.

> Folks who have forgotten the ways of our ancestors,
> Have forgotten themselves.

"And so, some folks listened and liked what the sage had to say, and some criticized for reminding them of the old ways; and many others even hated him for it. But he understood right from the start that it won't be easy to change all folks' hearts, since every man's heart is unique in its own vainglorious way; and those who refused to believe that they might need a lot more work on themselves to remove the stone from their hearts so they could change their ways continued to walk on the same path following their own ways.

"The teachings of our ancestors continue to thrive till this very day, as the fundamental practice has not changed.

"Those who welcomed and followed the ways that the sage reminded folks removed the stone from their hearts, filled their minds with peace and love, and their souls with joy; and continued to pass the ways of our ancestors from soul to soul as it reached mine and now yours."

I thanked *starúshku* (a little old lady) for passing on the teachings of the ways of our ancestors to me. I promised her that I will keep them in my thoughts.

I walked back up the mountain through the same narrow path that led me to the log cabin and the sequoia tree. I stopped and stood for a moment admiring the Mother Earth that revealed herself to me with all her gorgeous nature. I took a few deep breaths in and heavily exhaled the last one, followed by a sudden thought that dawned upon me.

> If your goal is to climb to the top of the mountain
> Then the mountain is your limit,
> If your goal is to reach the sky
> Then the sky is your limit,
> But if your goal is to pass the mountain and the sky,
> And enter into the universe
> Then you have no limit,
> For your limit becomes like the universe
> That never stops to expand and evolve.

ARTEM VASKANYAN

Day VII
Small Creatures

I saw monks and practitioners heading to the garden to practice walking meditation and followed them. I walked with them calmly and peacefully until the sun appeared directly above me, making me feel small and irrelevant in this world. And whether I like to admit to myself or not; I am but a small creature after all, just as many other living creatures that crawl under my feet here on Mother Earth.

> Little things in life are easily missed
> They cannot be seen by an untrained eye.
> It takes a man with an open mind to fully grasp
> That it is the smallest things in life
> That matter the most.

> Who am I to say that the lives
> That crawl under my feet
> Are less valuable than the one I see
> By my trained eye.
> I might just go ahead and say
> That folks who come from unfamiliar places
> Their lives are less important to the ones
> Who are well-known to us.

I was once that small creature who was discarded by the so-called "justice" system in a place where *mayá zhízn* (my life) was insignificant, irrelevant to the ones with an untrained eye; and where men in the position of power did as they wished with *zékami* (prisoners) for they looked at them as small creatures who did not deserve to walk amongst them.

For years I've been embarrassed, ashamed to say to anyone who asked me how many years I'd been sentenced to. I always hated that question. One thing that you never ask another *zek* (prisoner) is how many years he is serving. That is the most offensive question, even worse than being asked, "What you here for?" by someone you never met before. The last thing that any *zek* ever wants is to be reminded of how many more years he has to be in this *dyer'mé* (shit-hole). For me it was not only that, but instead that I was more embarrassed of talking about my *tyurémskam srókye* (prison sentence) than of the nature of my crime or being reminded where I still am. And when I would tell *zékam* (convicts) that the judge gave me a screamer for stealing a box of jewelry, every *zek* that heard about it was shocked and in disbelief.

"What! For that *huyinyú* (bullshit)? Pedophiles and rapists and murderers get less time than you!" they would all say to me. I knew that was true and that was what pissed me off because the system thought of me as worse than those *pédiki, nasílsheki, yí ubítzi* (pedophiles, rapists, and killers). Most of the comments that I would hear were from the violent career criminals who for the most part were serving much less time than I was. They often would say to me, "It is crazy how the system screwed you over!" Unfortunately, I was not the only one who was screwed by the "justice" system, and the more time I've spent *v tyur'mé* (in prison) the more people I've met who were just like me, a small creature who got screwed by the so-called "justice" system that wasn't so just after all, at least not for prisoners. It was as if the scales of justice were broken for the accused, tilted only to one side to benefit only the prosecutors.

To get a severe sentence, it all depends on who the crime is committed against; how expensive your lawyer is; are you cooperating with *mentámi* (the cops) and are you willing to become their *sukayi* (bitch); how hard is the prosecutor gunning for you to make a career out of your case; is the jury open-minded; and does the judge have *sérdze* (a heart). All of these factors essentially determine if you are going *v tyur'mú* (to prison) for a couple of years or a couple of decades.

Right from the start everything in my case was going *k chórtu* (to hell) for me. The box of jewelry that I'd stolen happened to belong to some politician's mistress. The same politician who preached, "More time for crime," and who was fighting to bring down the Italian and Russian organized crime. My so-called "*zver*" (the beast) attorney who was just as expensive an hour as were the shoes that he wore and who cost me all of my money that I had saved up, including my *mátushkyi* (mother's). But in the end, he turned out to be the biggest sellout working for the DA's office rather than for the clients. He worked with the prosecutors to pick and choose who gets a deal, loses, or beats a trial. At the beginning he was so vociferous and aggressive with the prosecutor that I really thought that he was *zver* like everyone said that he was, but after he got paid and the trial started, he became as quiet as *m'ish* (a mouse), never objecting to anything that was concocted against me by *mentámi* (the cops) and falsely presented evidence by the prosecutor. At first, I thought it was his strategy; but what did I know!

Ya nekagdá v prablémye s zakónam nye bil. (I've never been in trouble with the law.) I didn't understand how the whole process worked, and the lawyer who got paid never defended me like he was supposed to.

There was no other option for me but to go to trial, especially when the F.B.I. found out who my uncle was. They tried to make me flip on him and help them build a case against him and essentially to bury him *v tyur'mé* (in prison). I could've had the entire case against me dropped. All I had to do was to turn into a snake, the same *zmiyú* (snake) that my friend turned into when he sold me out down the river. All I had to do was to bring the box of jewelry to my uncle and hand it to him. But when I said to the cops, "I don't know what you're talking about! What box? I have never seen this box in my life! And if I had this much jewelry, I wouldn't be living in this shit hole! Someone must've planted it. And one more thing! I don't have an uncle! Just because we happen to both be Russians it doesn't mean that we are related and part of the Russian organized crime! That is just racist! You should all be ashamed of yourselves!"

Anyway, that was the defense that I used. I had nothing else to work with but that. The F.B.I. and the prosecutor didn't like my answers. They took it personally and wanted to make an example out of me and make sure that I would go *v tyur'mú* (to prison) for a very long time. I wanted to plead guilty, but the deal that was offered to me was 20 years, the same amount of years that I was facing if I were to lose at trial. It made no sense to plead guilty. I rolled the dice, but the house always wins. I lost way before the trial even began.

At trial the jury looked like they really hated me right from the start. All of them turned out to be relatives to someone in the police force. With the cops' mentality, they must've been thinking, "If he is here on trial, then he must be guilty of the crime, otherwise the cops would've never arrested him." But the reason that they did arrest me was because of my friend who told *mentám* (the cops) that it was I who robbed that place and that the jewelry box was still in my house.

The trial started after the sunrise and before it would set, I was already found guilty. It was the fastest trial known in world history. The prosecutor was so happy that I was found guilty that she was high-fiving all of the cops behind her with big smiles on their faces because she knew that by putting away another Russian criminal/immigrant it would give her the promotion that she was waiting for. It will make her career. In the end, it was all about building their careers and making a name for themselves on the backs of the criminals. And the judge looked like he wanted to get this over with so bad, and as quickly as he could, he rendered his sentence of 20 years right after the guilty verdict was read; and as I was handcuffed and quickly walked out of the courtroom, I heard him making plans for dinner, saying to the prosecutor and my "beast" attorney, "Well, now, let's go get dinner at the Mama Mia! I think it's on me this time."

When the judge said that I will be *v tyur'mé* (in prison) for 20 years, I thought he was joking. But as he continued to talk, I realized that he was as serious as my face was. My heart dropped and I felt a quiver going through my body, and as I turned around, I saw my *mátushka* behind me in tears. And behind her the two F.B.I. detectives were laughing and hugging each other.

I was more sad than upset that the "justice" system never even tried to understand why the crime occurred. And why would a 19-year-old kid be involved in criminal activities? To the prosecutor and the cops, it was irrelevant whether the criminal intent was there or not. In their eyes, if the crime happened then there must be *tyurémskiyi srok* (the prison sentence), and not just any sentence, but a draconian one where the perpetrator will be put away for as long as possible. For them this was justice; and especially for a criminal who was an immigrant. They must've been thinking, "Who the fuck does this guy think he is coming to our country and committing a crime against our own! We have to make an example out of him or there will be others following his footsteps." And that they did!

For 20 long years I would wake up and go to sleep with the number 20 etched into my mind; and for the first few years everywhere that I went to, the chow hall, gym, library, even when I watched T.V. or read or wrote, I thought of nothing but *mayóm srókye* (my sentence). This made me become psychologically depleted and feel insignificant in this world. Like I didn't even exist. To me it was a death sentence. I never believed that the 20 years would actually pass, and if they did, I would never see the end of it *zhivím* (alive). Every day I thought of how many years more I had left to serve; and not so much about the crime that I had committed because, let's face it, the crime did not match the punishment, and because of that it defeated the entire purpose of why I was *v tyur'mé* (in prison) in the first place. Refusing to cooperate with the cops and become their *stukachóm* (informant) and not for the crime that I was guilty of, that was the true reason of my severe sentence. I was someone who they could not manipulate and control to their advantage.

For many years I felt ashamed telling people how many years I was sentenced to by the system, but then I realized that I wasn't embarrassed for me, but for the entire "justice" system who so mercilessly decided to bury me without even trying to understand the reason for my wicked action; but instead tried to exploit me and take advantage of my vulnerable situation simply because I tried to preserve the value of my moral principles, and not so much to other people, but to myself. I ultimately paid for it with my life. I always valued the essence of my soul more than anything else in my life including my own freedom, and I could not allow myself to go down that road where it would pollute my soul beyond repair.

Do not believe when you hear that the sole existence of prisons is to change *zékav* (prisoners) for the better. It is to change them, that part is true! Only not for the better, but rather to further destroy them, to tear them down internally, to shred every living particle that makes them human until there is nothing left in them to go on with life, and that is the true reason for the existence of *tyur'm* (the prisons) and the goal of the men in positions of power.

Men in a position of power haven't forgotten how to do their job, and that is why they are good at what they do; and the angrier the men in power are, the harsher the treatment of *zékav* is *v tyur'máh* (in prisons).

> When an angry, unstable person
> Is placed in a position of power
> Nothing good will ever come from it,
> Only turmoil and disorder will arise
> Amongst the people.
> Those who found themselves
> In a position of power to govern prisons,
> Instead of encouraging prisoners to pursue
> Their path to constructive behavior
> Did everything within their power
> To discourage prisoners to improve their lives;
> Their hatred for prisoners is greater
> Than the good that exists within them,
> And because of that they look at prisoners as small creatures,
> And livestock to financially profit from;
> Rather than as human beings

Who are in need of support and guidance.

To attain any positive growth for any man can only be achieved by their own desire and relentless work on themselves. Every *zek* eventually found a way to escape the suffocating prison walls that were instilled in him by angry, unstable men in a position of power, even if it meant in a process of such escapism tearing one's *dúshu na chásti* (soul apart).

Throughout most of my time in prison, despite how bad it was, I felt blessed that I'd fallen in love with writing *poém'yi* (poetry) instead of intoxicants or other vices like gambling and self-destructive behaviors. I can proudly say that writing *poém'yi* pulled my soul out of misery. It gave me an ability to understand myself better along with developing internal growth and wisdom. However, the more my wisdom grew and internally transformed my inner nature, the freer my mind became, and the more agony increased in my soul from realizing that I was not living in accord to my human nature, which was to experience *zhízn* (life) the fullest, even if I was a small creature living under control by the men in a position of power who did not believe that I deserved to exist amongst them.

> I often wonder!
> Why did Creator keep me alive for all these years?
> For what reason?
> I couldn't understand with all the power of my mind.
> All my Creator ever did for me was to take and take
> Until there was nothing left in me.
> And then I just stopped caring!
> I stopped craving!
> For there was nothing and no one else left to care for…
> I guess life simply ain't fair!
> No one ever does get what he really desires in the end.
> Even when I gained a little, that little came with a price.
> Since with time my knowledge, and then my wisdom, grew
> So did the sorrow unbearably increase.
> The wisdom that came into my life
> It filled my heart with hope and joy
> And gave a purpose to my life;

> But the sorrow that came with it,
> Kept pinching my soul from realizing that
> Life can never be satisfied fully to the end.
> Not the way I craved at least.
> And so I wonder!
> Why did Creator keep me alive for all these years?
> FOR WHAT REASON?

At times my pain was so heavy on my heart that I would wish that I would've stayed in that blissful ignorance where I had no worries of what transpired in this world and within *chelavécheskayi dushé* (a human soul); but once I left that state of mind, I could never return to it again, since once I saw the light, I no longer was attracted to *timnatyé* (the darkness). It was as if my life-giving force, the spirit, had transformed my moral principles, the soul, to the point of no return to those old ways again.

Many *zéki* (convicts) who found a way to thrive *v tyur'mé* (in prison) thought that they would do the same once they were released. Not only were they wrong, but also delusional, untouched with reality. After being *v tyur'mé* for half of their lives, many gained all the necessary life experience to survive in the dark places, but had none when it came to living outside the prison walls, since just as it took them time to get used to the life in prison, they needed even more time to snap out of a long-time imprisoned mentality since they were released, which was the hardest part of it all, since I still struggle with it to this day.

Many *zéki*, including myself, dreamed of building a house, opening a business, and becoming someone important without understanding that a great amount of knowledge, time, and sweat are required to accomplish such goals; and accomplishing such dreams are impossible for *zékam* (prisoners) who did nothing but *huinyóyi-stradáli* (bull-shitted) their entire bid.

Most of my time I vigorously read and wrote *poém'yi* (poetry), where I found my inspiration from misery, despair, and hope. I managed to accumulate wisdom and internal growth from that, but not as much knowledge as I was hoping to. That particular element was extremely important to help me survive and become successful outside *tyurémskih styén* (the prison walls). However, it was close to none. I recognize that

I lacked then as I lack now this key component of how to put together my ideas, since knowledge is knowing, while wisdom is knowing how to apply that knowledge. But when you have no knowledge, wisdom cannot be applied, since there is nothing to apply it to.

Many *zéki* (convicts) such as myself found themselves in exactly the same predicament, and it was for one particular reason that men in a position of power who governed prisons did everything that they possibly could to limit and prevent prisoners from earning their education and all the necessary skills that they would need to help them find work once they were released.

During my time in prison my goal became to publish *kaléktzíyu poém* (the collection of poems) that I spent my entire prison bid crafting. I wanted to publish my work of art by the time my prison sentence would come to an end, since I was skeptical of myself if I would actually pursue my goal at the end as a free man, since the truth is I am just like everyone else, not the same person outside *tyurémskih styén*, just as I am completely different while being on the inside. Besides, it would be an unimaginable feeling to have my dream come true in a place that was designed to work against all *zékav* (prisoners). I figured if I could achieve this task of publishing my book while being *v tyur'mé* (in prison) then imagine what I could do once I was released! And since I knew that the existence of the prisons was to make sure that every *zek* would fail at his positive growth, I wanted to prove to the men in positions of power that you may have the power to keep me behind the walls, but you don't have the power to tell me how I should do my time, that part is entirely up to me.

At first, I couldn't understand why in God's name would *tyurémskaya administrátziya* (the prison administration) try to interfere in prisoners' positive growth. What do they have to gain by that? Especially when they claimed that they encourage positive growth amongst all *zékav* (prisoners); but then, as I was trying to make payment to the publishing company for their publishing services to self-publish my book, they would not only freeze my account, but also opened an investigation on me where they would read my mail, listen to my phone calls, like I was involved in illegal activities selling *narkatú* (drugs) or something. However, the truth was that *zéki* (convicts) who pushed themselves to transform their lives for the better, who managed to educate themselves, were always looked upon by the men in positions of power as a threat to their system, since educated *zéki* have an ability to challenge the prison system and expose their abuse of power that is occurring within *tyurémskih styén* (the prison walls); and most importantly, it is an educated *zek* who is less likely to come back *v tyur'mú* (to prison) and keep the recidivism low as well as enlighten other *zékav* (cons) to pursue the same positive path; and all of that essentially was bad for the prison business as a whole to grow stronger.

If *tyurémskaya admínistrátziya* (the prison administration) does not have every *zéka* (prisoner) on a short leash, controlling his every move, then they think that they are losing their grip on the prisoners and become closer at being exposed for their systematic abuse of power. Not only did they intentionally not provide education to prisoners, but they also deliberately prevented them from pursuing it on their own through mail correspondence. *Tyurémskaya admínistrátziya* is directly responsible for lessening prisoners' chances to become successfully employed once they were released, in the process leaving many of them in even worse shape financially, and most importantly, psychologically than when they entered into prison. Without money, work skills, being psychologically traumatized, and more angry than they ever were before, many leave prison empty-handed, since not every *zek* has family to rely on for support. The entire process by *tyurémskayi admínistrátziyeyi* (the prison administration) was nothing more than a setup right from the start for *zékam* (prisoners) to fail outside the prison walls.

Zéki (Convicts) who spent decades in prison without being close to their wives/women unequivocally were psychologically affected by the loneliness and despair on an indescribable level. It is unnatural for *muzhikú* (a man) to be without a woman for so long. Even little things such as having access to the cable R-rated movies, contact visits, smut magazines, or a razor to shave with, all of it was restricted by the men in positions of power with only one purpose on their mind, to further torment *zékav* (prisoners). Can you imagine serving decades or a life sentence without ever having access to a little comfort, as if *zéki* are not even human beings? And then once released to be suddenly expected to act as a normal human being like all of these psychological tortures have never even happened? I can only say from my own personal experience that after being treated like a machine for 20 years, normal is never possible. I can only pretend to act like I'm normal. I am not angry, but only sad for the tormentors because as human beings they are not only lost but confused; and

>Confused people don't know the difference
>Between money and their souls.
>They would rather reveal their most soulful moments
>Of their lives to complete strangers
>Than give money to them.
>Confused people value all the wrong things in life.
>They value money more than their own souls
>As if money has greater value than
>Their precious souls which were given to them for nothing
>Before they were even born.

Many of *zéki* (the prisoners) who were finally released after being demoralized and tormented by the men in positions of power went back to their old ways; and not only out of desperation to make a living, but from the psychological trauma that they endured while being *v tyur'mé* (in prison) for a lingering period of time. Greed is the reason why the men in positions of power become cruel to prisoners, since each prison employs at least a thousand guards, also case workers, medical staff. And it's because of *zékav* (prisoners) that these employees have high-paying jobs. Not to mention the court system that has parole/probation officers, attorneys, judges, bailiffs who all depend on *zékav* to keep coming back to prison to make their careers, especially for the cops whose sole existence depends on *zékav* recommitting their crimes. The "justice" system is like a giant fishpond where everyone who works for the system comes to feed on the small fish who happen to be *zéki* (the prisoners); and at the end of each meal as *zéki* get greedily devoured by the entire "justice" system, they are being hated by them. It is a vicious cycle that just does not end, like the lives of small creatures in this world do not even matter as they are taken for granted by the big creatures who are so blatantly ignorant to realize that their entire existence depends on the survival of the small creatures.

ARTEM VASKANYAN

DAY VII
THE MIND

I stopped and stood without thinking as everyone continued to move along the path like clouds above my head. My mind froze. I felt as if I had burned all of my brain cells out with all the heavy burden that I carry with me from the past. It's been three months and a week now since I've been released. Perhaps it's time to move on from all of this *gavná* (shit) that I keep thinking about *dyén'yi noch'* (day and night) relentlessly.

A known shadow to my eyes appeared in front of me. My *diadía* (uncle) Yúra was standing behind me and looking at me. He must've seen how much I've drifted from this place into a place that was well-known to him, for I stood without twitching a muscle for a minute now.

We walked calmly as we conversed, for it was our last day together;

and we both mutually felt as if we had to take advantage of what time was left and share our life's moments before I would depart tomorrow early in the morning.

He said, "Ever since my true practice has begun, I worked on myself *dyén'yi noch'* so I would not go back to the obstacles of material life that I left behind; and so desperately missed and craved day after day and night after night.

"The money and the power, manipulation and control, and all *krasív'yiye zhénshin'yi* (the beautiful women), the delicious food, the game of the hustle, and all other seductive parts of life that attracts and pollutes the mind and turns all men into an empty shell.

"I craved it and missed it for that polluted *zhízn* (life), since my mind had not been cleansed in the clear water. It took a great deal of time, and most importantly, patience along with daily practice to get rid of all the dirty thoughts that etched into my mind from living a polluted *zhízn* ever since I could recall.

"There was a time in my life when I once thought that I found a way to flourish in places where most folks perished; and I was proud of that, until I asked myself a simple question: at what cost!

"Since I had managed to survive in such a way that in the end it left my mind in a state of total wretchedness, it made me stop believing that I could ever have a chance to live a normal *zhízn* again.

"I managed to come so far in life because I finally realized what that polluted *zhízn* was doing to my mind. I applied the teachings into my practice and only then I understood that,

> The mind is like a sponge,
> If you were to soak it in dirty water
> Then the sponge will absorb dirt,
> And it will become part of the sponge;
> And the only way to remove the dirt
> Is to cleanse it in the clear water,
> And that is the only way
> To keep your mind clean.

"And ever since my practice began, I stopped reaching for the parts of life that pollute my mind, for I knew how easy it was to fall back into my old ways, just like many other folks who had perished just as fast as they had flourished simply because they have forgotten that the practice never ends. It is an ongoing journey for the rest of our lives.

"You have to be very careful
The way you treat your mind,
For the mind is like a fragile flower
All it takes is one ill-use
For the petals to fall off.
Watch out for the parasites,
And not the animals or the plants
That leech on to survive,
But for the human beings who do it purely
Out of wicked heart, mind, and soul
Which is much worse than of an animal and plant.
A man who harbors a soul of a parasite
Survives on the generosity of kind people.
It takes for granted everything good
That has been done and said to it.
It mooches, scrounges, sponges, and drains
The energy out of strong and young,
As it leeches on to see good folks fail,
And won't ever stop until they fall
From being drained to their last drop of blood.
And the only way to fight these parasites is,
First you have to realize who is in your life,
And then, cut off the leech entirely from your life.
And that is the only way to keep your mind clean and safe,
And keep all the parasites at bay along with all pollution
That you had been attracted to,
Before you realized what caused
A flower's petals to fall off."

ARTEM VASKANYAN

Day VII
Last Supper

I had zero appetite during supper. I was still full from lunch that I'd insatiably devoured. I figured I'd let *kashalót* (the sperm whale) enjoy eating for both of us on our last day. The only thing that I grabbed was a cup of tea with a spoon of honey and a slice of lemon.

I sat peacefully like I had no worries in the world and slowly sipped *móyi cháyi* (my tea) and thought to myself of how *sesshin* was coming to an end just as quickly as it had begun; and how after all the pains and sufferings that I had endured as they had etched into my mind and made me deeply grieve; nonetheless, I felt as if I was destined to end up on this path that I have out of ignorance been avoiding most of my life. All for one purpose, I suppose, to end up in this old monastery with my *díadía* Yúra as a guide, where I could reinvent myself as a new *chelavék* (man).

I don't know if it was my heart or if a monk slipped something into *móyi cháyi* (my tea) that made me feel a great deal of forgiveness for anyone who caused me harm throughout my life; and not because of kindness and compassion that I seemed to develop in my heart during these enlightening, ruminating days; but because of understanding that people are not always conscious of what they do and say, just like I once wasn't.

After all this time I finally started to look at myself as being a rough, precious stone being polished and cut out of its impurities; and not as some piece of useless rock, like I've been treated all my life.

> For years I felt like I was a dried-up plant
> Sitting in the middle of the desert,
> And waiting for the rain to come;
> And when I finally realized
> That it will never come,
> My roots began to extend further
> Deep down into the earth in search of the water
> Like the roots of a grapevine,
> Until they reached a hidden well;
> And then I suddenly began to spring back to life
> And feel more alive
> Than I ever had in my entire life;
> Until I could stand up on my own two feet,
> And say, I've been reborn!

My *diadía* placed a plate of rice with vegetables on the table and sat by my side and said, "*Ya óchen' tabóyi garzhús* (I am very proud of you) for going through to the end of the retreat and taking it all with seriousness like your life depended on it! I know it wasn't easy, and after tonight's meditation you have successfully completed the *sesshin*, and you should be proud yourself. I know I am!

"*Da! Ya rád* (Yes! I'm glad) that I stayed with it to the end, but I still have no control over my arising thoughts that causes me to dwell on the past that I so desperately want to leave behind," I said.

"*Da!* The Buddhist practice does that a lot. It really makes you dig deep down into the core of *tvayéyi dushí* (your soul) and reevaluate your life in a way it was never done before.

"And it makes you find the courage that you never knew you had within yourself. Remember that Buddhism is not for cowards. It is for those who wish to develop a strong will and who are not afraid to look into their *sérdze* (hearts) and dig into the hearts of their *dush* (souls); and bring out and face the guilt and shame that they hid out of sight and out of pride.

"The entire practice stresses on improving your awareness through the practices that you have experienced during *sesshin*; to become aware when the mind drifts, whether to the past or the future; to find the willpower to let the fantasies, regrets, pleasant and hurtful memories that cause your mind to drift away from reality, dissipate and always come back to the breath for a fresh start.

"Remember that the past is not real, it is only a memory to be taken, learned from, and let go of. Your actions from the past do not define who you are, it is what you do with yourself right now that will reveal who you truly are.

"In the end, it just doesn't matter how your life began, all that matters now is how it will come to an end. And everything that you are trying to accomplish can only be achieved on your own, just as you have managed it since the *sesshin* has begun.

"Overall, the guidance that you received on your path are nothing more than tools for you to apply to your daily life once you leave.

> "Life does not have to feel
> Like every day you are heading into the fray,
> Where you fight to your last breath to survive.
> Life does not have to be full of suffering,
> Where you are choking on anger and revenge.
> Life does not have to be a dark place,
> Where you are constantly searching for the light.
> Life can be simple, calm, and peaceful,
> And full of joy."

ARTEM VASKANYAN

Day VII
Patience

That night every practitioner including myself at the *zendo* sat motionless and attentively listening to *roshi*'s last teachings. I cannot speak for every practitioner, but I felt extremely proud of myself to come to the end of such a profound, self-enlightening, and brief experience in my life during these seven days. When *roshi* spoke, he seemed delighted at the way *sesshin* went.

"I am glad that everyone so diligently took part in the Buddhist *Zen* practice," he said. "However, I would like to end the night and the *sesshin* with one last teaching that I haven't discussed as of yet.

"I am talking about the most important quality that all men struggle within themselves to develop, and that without it nothing tangible can be accomplished in life.

"All of our goals depend on us being patient with ourselves, since with patience we can discover how real problems are when they arise prior to reacting to them, especially in a way that we will regret later.

"When we don't fully grasp the cause of the arising situation and react to it spontaneously, then we ignore considering the consequences of our reactions to the problem, which will only prolong our sufferings and cause the problem to arise again.

"Reacting with anger to the unpleasant situations does more harm to us than it does to the protagonists, since with time anger subsides and we can start to see more clearly how to approach the problem in a less aggressive way and resolve it with calm and, hopefully, peace; instead of escalating the situation with our harsh words and actions.

"It is only with patience that we can transform the way we think of how to deal with arising problems; and make ourselves realize that problems are simply part of life, and that they will always arise and cause us to suffer.

"However, by keeping in mind that nothing in this world is permanent and that all problems in life with time will pass, it will help us understand that all we need to do is be patient.

"Patience is more important to our development than we might even imagine, since every goal that we try to achieve in our life requires of us to be patient.

"If we want to find our purpose in this world;
Cultivate mental growth; improve our practice;
Be still and silent; interconnect with our spiritual growth;
Become awakened to our higher level of wisdom;
Understand ourselves and everything that revolves around us;
We must first learn how to be patient.
We must understand that,
When we give up on our goals, we lack perseverance;
When we avoid work, we lack diligence;
When we are aggravated, we lack tolerance;
When we cannot control our temper, we lack equanimity;
When we have no self-control, we lack forbearance;
When we feel hatred, we lack love;
When we seek revenge, we lack forgiveness;

When we are ungrateful, we lack appreciation;
When we cannot endure pain, we lack endurance;
When we feel suffering, we lack joy;
When we cannot see what others see, we lack understanding;
When we live in oblivion, we lack mindfulness;
When we are ignorant, we lack knowledge;
When we act like idiots, we lack wisdom;
When we feel internally empty, we lack spiritual growth;
But what we truly lack is patience."

I sat with the *sangha*, a group of monks and practitioners, and ruminated on *roshi*'s words; of how patience was in fact an essential element in everyone's life. His words sparked a memory, reminding me when I was *v tyur'mé* (in prison) grappling within myself to defeat the hopeless moments of despair; and where for years I lacked that essential element to help me improve myself. Just from being there, it was already a robbery of my most precious commodity of my life, the time; and no matter what I did or how I served my time, time was always selfish. It was never on my side.

I realized that I had no control over time and that by getting frustrated about my incapacitated situation, I was only setting myself up for more failures. I suppose after I understood that part, it became clear that I had only two options in life: to succeed or give up, which meant to literally live or die; and dying was not appealing to my free spirit.

After being lost for years, I finally came up with, all on my own, a way to start building myself from the ground up. I usually don't like to boast about any of my accomplishments, but I ended up developing a way to improve my patience all on my own.

I guess what gave me the drive to start developing patience were the meaningless words said by people: "Have patience!" But none of them would ever explain how to achieve it. It was their ignorance that made me search and create a practice for myself where at the end of each day I had to accomplish something productive, no matter what it was, whether to write *poyému* (a poem), a short letter, read a few pages out of a book, and/or workout. I just had to do something that would make me feel good about myself. Eventually, I programmed myself to do that everyday and after a short while it started to get easier and fruitful, where from writing a short *poyému* (poem), it turned into an epic poem and then into a book of poetry; a short letter into many long letters; reading a few pages out of a book into reading an entire book in a few days; and a light workout into daily training.

> To have patience was like having a breath of fresh air.
> And when by the end of the day
> I did not achieve all of my daily goals,
> I would feel like I was being robbed
> Of that most essential element in my life,
> The time.

Day VII
The Way of the Spirit

That night I dreamed I was strolling through the dense forest under the moonlight until I reached an ancient temple hidden between two hillocks. The temple was surrounded by the ruins of many Buddha statues and instead of the roof, the temple had a clear sky with stars. The sudden sounds of men's yelps and the clashes of their swords echoed throughout the ancient temple. I looked inside the temple and there they were, two Shaolin monks fighting each other, each wielding a katana in their hands; and by the entrance of the temple stood an older monk with a long beard reaching down to his knees and watching them attentively compete.

The monk suddenly turned to me and without questioning who I was said, "When two fighters practice in the same way the same style of the martial art, then with time the art will grow in its own way in each one of them, and not because of their different body or mind, but because of the unique spirit that dwells within each one of them; and you may even say that the way a fighter fights is the way his spirit is. Calm with calmness. Angry with anger.

"The physical training and the mindful philosophy are factors in themselves to improve a fighter's skill; but the development of one's spiritual growth, the chi, which is the most fundamental aspect to the perfection of the martial art style within the fighter, is entirely a different factor in itself.

"No practitioner will ever be able to perfect the style of the martial art that he is studying unless he will train not only his body and mind, but also his spirit, the energy of life. For the practitioner the training of the internal growth, of the chi, is the most essential ingredient that will allow him to transform his practiced martial art style to the higher spiritual level.

"And when one day two fighters collide to battle each other to test their skills, it is not only their body and mind and the practiced martial art that is at war with each other, but also their spirits. Consequently, it is the fight between two spirits and not the fighters that will determine which one of them is the strongest.

"The martial arts are nothing more than just tools to help a practitioner find his way to the path where he could apply the studied art to his life and cultivate his chi to determine that it is not his martial art style that is being tested against his opponent, but his spirit.

"The superior fighter tests his practice by tapping into his chi, the energy of life, to merge all three elements, the body, the mind, and the spirit into one; and that is what is being tested here when two practitioners compete.

"All hellacious souls are forged
The same way as katanas
In the depths of the hell-fires,
Where no other elements known to Creator
Could ever withstand such hellacious hell-fires;
Until they are released into the realm of the living,

ZEK

Where they will be molded further by their masters,
Till they appear more beautiful
Than flowers on the highest mountains
And deadlier than the Reaper in the earthly realm.
Before the elements take a form of katana,
The sword maker forges its metals
In the depths of the furnace as hot as the hell-fires;
And as he molds the elements
He hammers them into one brick piece
And beats it and folds it endless times,
Until it stretches into a thin, long layer of metal sheet
In the shape of the sword;
And as soon as the sword maker pulls it out
From the furnace as hot as the hell-fire,
He quenches it in the cold water
That creates a curve in the sword;
He patiently sharpens the blade
And polishes every spot on the sword
For as long as it takes
To perfect his art of work;
And only when his soul is satisfied
With his work of art,
Does the sword transform into the katana;
And then its powers are tested
On the stack of bamboo,
As it must cut through
Like a knife goes through butter
For the sword to be finally called the katana;
And as for the spiritual force, the chi
That dwells within a man to be called a soul,
It must go through the similar molding process;
Where the soul must endure extreme pains and sufferings
As it did in the hellacious hell-fires,
And be patiently sharpened and polished
On the obstacles of life
Just like the precious elements

Found at the bottom of the mountains
And then molded, sharpened, and polished;
Until it has reached its perfection like katana,
And then tested within a man
In his own internal hell-fire.

Day VIII
Departure

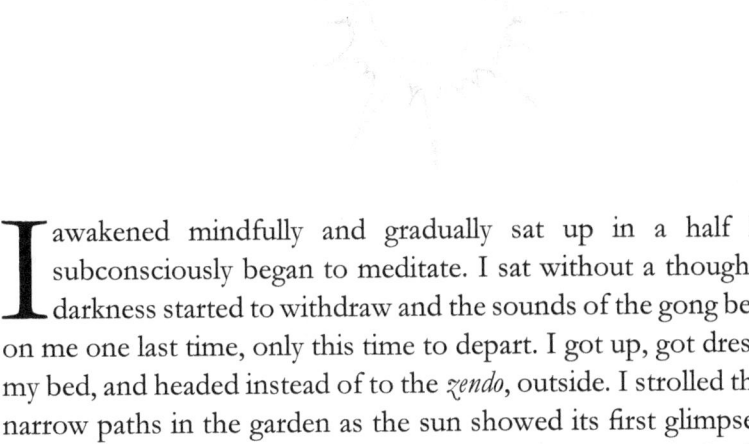

I awakened mindfully and gradually sat up in a half lotus and subconsciously began to meditate. I sat without a thought until the darkness started to withdraw and the sounds of the gong began to call on me one last time, only this time to depart. I got up, got dressed, made my bed, and headed instead of to the *zendo*, outside. I strolled through the narrow paths in the garden as the sun showed its first glimpses of light, revealing little bees pollinating flowers. The residue on the bushes' leaves and blades of grass left by last night's drizzle shone like tiny crystals when the rays of the sun stroked its leaflets; and the rest of the sentient beings suddenly emerged as they crawled out of their little homes, filling the garden's air space with the flying, buzzy insects bringing the entire garden back to life. And as the folks began to come out of their cells and out of the housing just like the insects did out of theirs, everything came to life around me within a few short breaths. The illuminating rays of the sun, the insects buzzing, the folks talking while departing, even the air that filled the garden changed and felt more alive, and I hadn't felt this way since I was young and free.

The illuminating rays of the sun warmed my skin and the gentle wind brushed up against my clothing; the evergreen trees swayed back and forth and the soft meadow that I stood on felt like my *dédushki* (grandfather's) Armenian carpet under my feet, and the sweet, aromatic smell from the clover flowers perfumed the air as the bees and dragonflies collected their nectar by my feet. The murder of crows flew over me, and the raven appeared hovering in the sky above me.

There is something amazing about this place and the people that right from the start made me feel connected to *mayéyi zhízni* (my life). *Sesshin* turned out to be something extraordinary. Something that I have never dreamed of experiencing. These seven days of retreat brought me not only out of my melancholy, but also helped me answer many mind-boggling questions, and most importantly, it gave me a sense of self-awareness, which I consider to be the most fundamental part that helped me to fully grasp parts of my suppressed life that I'd been grappling with boundlessly ever since I realized that the path that I was on just made no sense to me.

Manáhi (The monks) were chanting "Om mani padme hum…" as the practitioners were departing. My *diadía* and I both said, "*Prayshàyi!* (Goodbye!)" and hugged each other one last time; and as I was walking to the gates dressed in my worldly clothing, he caught up to me and said, "*Ne zabúd* (Don't forget) that,

> "Life is all about searching for something mysterious,
>   And then in the process of finding it
>   Becoming strong enough to let it go."

Part of me was glad that I was finally leaving and that now I had a chance to apply all that I had attained in my heart and mind to *mayéyi zhízni*, but the other part of me wanted to remain in this place where I found my peace and calm. I guess I had a perfect balance in me after all—a fear to fail and plenty of courage to test myself on my new path.

As I exited through the gates of the monastery, a feeling of déjà vu arose within me of that earth-shattering day when I was finally set free; and how there wasn't a single *dushá* (soul) that awaited me on the other side of the prison gates to welcome me into the world of the living that I hadn't felt nor seen for half of my life.

>And as I crossed to the other side,
>The same way as I crossed back then,
>But only through the giant gates of hell;
>I had a big smile on my face,
>But on the inside my heart was crying,
>My soul was bleeding,
>And my spirit was wounded
>From all that I had endured and lost;
>But now, it all feels like a distant dream
>Without any pain and loss.
>And although I'm alone in this free world,
>Without a family of my own,
>Nor enough money to live comfortably,
>Nor college education to help me get a better job,
>Yet, I feel rich
>As if my cup had been emptied
>And filled with rich Armenian red wine
>To the top.
>With Love,
>ZEK

Glossary

NOTE: In the spelling of the Russian words, I have provided transliteration of the Russian language. The best way to read and pronounce these words are in syllables and paying attention to the emphasis.

Glossary

Alkagóliku	(a) Drunk
Amitabha	(Buddha's name) Infinite light
Ana-shé-shú	Marijuana
Asá	(the/a) Wasp
Avalokitesvará	Is one of the three pure sages who exhibits the virtue of compassion, who dives into the deepest fire of hell to rescue beings from suffering.
Bábayagá	Witch
Bábushka	Grandmother
Baksyúr	Boxer
Bandít	(a) Thug
Ba-rán-ránom	Sheep (Stupid person)
Bó-g-ga	God
Bibliaté-ka-ku	Library
Bliad!	Shit!
Bólshye nikagdá	No more!
Brat-va-vóyi	Brotherhood/Comrades
Buddha	The enlightened one/Awakened
Buddhahood	The awakened mind/The enlightenment
Buddha-nature	The true unchanging and eternal nature of all beings that possess the seeds of Buddhahood (the awakened mind). The inherent potential in all beings to become a Buddha, the enlightened being.
Bukh-lá-ló-lú	Booze
Chelavé-k-ka-kam	(a) Man
Chelavécheskayi dushé	(a) Human soul
Chu-dakóm-dachkí	Bozo/Weirdo
Chérez ad	Through hell
Da!	Yes!
Da! Ya rad	Yes! I'm glad
Davéria	Trust
Dédush-ka–(ki)	Grandfather ('s)
Déngi	Money

Dermóvaya d'irá	Shithole
Dermóvim chelavékam	(a) Shitbag
Dharma	Buddha's teachings
Díadía (Yúra)	Uncle (Yúra)
Diávolam	(the) Devil
Díkih zveryéyi	Wild beasts
Díkiyi zver	(a) Wild beast
D'iryé	(a) Hole/Segregation block
Dóbraye!	Morning!
Dóbraye *útra*!	Good morning!
Droog	(a) Friend
Droog *íli* brat	Friend or brother
Drooz'yámi	Friends
Durák!	Idiot!
Durakí	Fools/Idiots
Duh	Spirit
Dush	Souls
Du-shá -shí -shóyi	Soul
Dushé yi dúhu	Soul and spirit
D*ú*shu na chásti	Soul apart
Dyén yi noch'	Day and night
Dyer'mé	Shithole
Ésli chésno!	To be frank!
Ésli chésno tho net!	To be honest, no!
Ésli skazát' právdu	To tell the truth
Éto dólgaya istória	It's a long story
Ex-zek	Ex-convict/Ex-con

Five Precepts   Not killing; Not stealing; Not misusing the senses; Not lying; and Not misusing intoxicants

Four Noble Truths   The existence of suffering; The causes of suffering; The cessation of the causes of suffering; The path that leads to the cessation of the causes of suffering.

Gav-ná -nó	Shit
Glú-pim -pami	(a) Fool/Fools
Glúpayi rózhayi	Dumb face
Gólim shlyúham	(the) Naked whores

ZEK

Haróshuyu Kármu	Good karma
Huyinyú	Bullshit/Crap
Huyinyóyi stradáli	Bullshitted
Ih dúhav	Their souls
Izbú	(the) Log cabin
Iz tyur'mí	From prison
Izvení	Sorry
Jukpi	A wooden stick used for meditation session
Kak tí	How are you
Kaléktziyu payém	(the) Collection of poetry
Kárma	Actions that lead to your reward in the future
Kasha-lót -lóta	Sperm whale
Kastét	Knuckle-duster
Ka-zyól -zlyé	Good for nothing/Loser
K chórtu	To hell
K svayéyi zhízni	To your life
Krasívami zhénshinami	Beautiful women
Krasívayi bábayi	(a) Beautiful broad
Krasívyiye zhénshin'yi	(the) Beautiful women
Klét-ka -ku	(a/the) Cage
Klét-ki -kah	(the) Cages
Kretína	(an) Idiot
Krísyi	Rats/Informants
Lyubóv'	Love
Manáh	(a) Monk
Maná-hi -ham -hov	Monks
Mátush-ka –	(ki) Mother ('s)
Mayá dushá yi móyi duh	My soul and my spirit
Mayá zhízn	My life
Mayá dushá	My spirit
Mayéyi bratvóyi	My brotherhood
Mayéyi dushé	My soul
Mayéyi dushí yi dúha	My soul and spirit
Mayéyi stárayi bratvóyi	My old brotherhood
Mayéyi zhízni	My life
Mayí glazá	My eyes

Mayími drooz'yámi	My friends
Mayóm sérdze	My heart
Mayóm srókye	My sentence
Mayú véru	My faith
Ment	Cop/Guard
Men-tám -támi -tóv	Cops/Guards
M'ish	(a) Mouse
Moksha	Liberation from the cycle of reincarnation of suffering
Móyi cháyi	My tea
Móyi droog, móyi brat	My friend, my brother
Móyi sín	My son
Móyi lútshiyi droog	My best friend
Móyi narkótik	My drug
Moyí bratánam	My brother
Moyím dróógam yi brátam	My friend and brother
Muzhi-ká -kú	(a) Man
Nachéyi	Nights
Nakarmí menyá!	Feed me!
Namaste	Expression on meeting or parting (When used as a greeting it means seeing the essence of one's inner being present within)
Na mayú zhízn	Upon my life
Narka-tá -tú -tyé	Drug
Narkamánu	Drug addict
Narkótik	(a) Drug
Násha daróga k prasveshéniyu	Our path to enlightenment
Nasílschiki	Rapists
Nastayáshiyi *ád*	(a) True hell
Nyeudáchnikami	Losers
Ne zabúd'	Don't forget
Nirvana	Reincarnation in the pure land of a total extinction of desires, pain, and suffering
(The) Noble Eightfold Path	(Is the Fourth Noble Truth) Wisdom, Morality, and Meditation
Nozh	(a) Knife
No znáyesh chto!	But you know what!
No ya bil ne prav!	But I was wrong!

Nu a seyichás	But now
Nu da!	That's right! (Well yeah!)
Oh! Pizdétz!	Oh! Shit! (Oh! Fuck!)
Oh mani padme hum	(The mantra) The Absolute that is contained in everything (those who find themselves in the deepest hell recite the mantra)
Óvashi yi frúkti	Vegetables and fruits
Pa-hán -hanóm	The boss
Pahán bratví	Boss of the brotherhood
Paká!	Bye!
Pavér' mnyé!	Trust me! (Believe me!)
Pédiki, nasilsheki, yi ubitzi	Pedophiles, rapists, and killers
Pedofíli	Pedophiles
Pídarami	(the) Chicken hawks/Gays
Píva	Beer
Poyému	(a) Poem
Poyém'yi	Poetry
Póhuyi	Fuck it!
Polnuyu lunú	The full moon
Po Rúskyi	In Russian
Prasháyi!	Goodbye!
Prasveshéni-ya -ye	Enlightenment
Prastí minyá	Forgive me
Právda	Truth
Pridál minyá	Betrayed me
Pridátel'stvu	Betrayal
Privét!	Hi!
Prízrak	(a) Ghost
Pustím chelavékam	(an) Empty man
Rabámi	Slaves
Rasíyu	Russia
Restarána	Restaurant
Roshi	The Japanese Zen master
Rúskayi kriminál'nayi organizáziyi	Russian criminal organization
Rúskayi organizóvaniyi prestúpnosti	Russian organized crime
Rúskiyi	Russian

Sabáka	(a) Dog
Samadhi	A state of total meditation in which the mind rests without wavering as it becomes one with oneself, (pure concentration) a state in which the mind is free from all distractions as it fully becomes observed in itself.
Samsara	Perpetual endless cycle of birth, death, and rebirth
Sangha	The community of the dharma followers, the monks, the nuns, and the Buddhist practitioners
S atkrítam sérdzam	With an open heart
Sérd-za -ze	Heart
Segaréti	Cigarettes
Sériyi volk	(a) Grey wolf
sesshin	A seven-day retreat
Shlyúha	(a) Whore
Shlyú-h -hi -hami	Whores
Sibíri	Siberia
Slísh'	Listen
Slúshayi	Listen
Slúshayi menyá	Listen to me
Smyért' ili tyur'má	Death or prison
Spakoínayi nóchi!	Good night!
Spasíba!	Thanks!
S.S.S.R.	U.S.S.R.
Stukachóm	Informant
Starichók	Little old man
Stáriyi chyórt	Old bastard
Starúshku	(a) Little old lady
Súka!	Bitch!
Súkayi	Bitch
Súkin sín	Son of a bitch
Svabódu	Freedom
Svabódyen	Free
Svyét	(the) Light
Ti chto dúmayesh!	What do you think!
Ti chto za'bíl	Did you forget
Ti menyá chut' ne pribíl	You almost took me out

Timnatyé	(the) Darkness
Ti *óchen* prável'na rasuzhdáyesh	You're thinking in the right way
Ti prav!	You are right!
Ti znáyesh!	You know!
Ti znáyesh chto díadía!	You know what uncle!
Tólka tyur'má *íli* smert'	Only prison or death
Tvayéyi dush*í*	Your soul
(The) Triple Jewel	The Buddha; The Dharma; The Sangha
Tróika	Trio
Tupáya asá	Stupid wasp
Tvayóm sérdze	Your heart
Tyemnatóyi	Darkness
Tyúr'm	(the) Prisons
Tyur'-má -mé -mú	Prison
Tyúr'm v Rasíye	Prisons in Russia
Tyurémskam srókye	Prison sentence
Tyrémskii mentí	(the) Prison Guards
Tyurémskami vrachámi	(the) Prison doctors
Tyurémskayu yédu	Prison food
Tyurémskaya admínistrátziya	(the) Prison administration
Tyurémskayi admínistrátziyeyi	(the) Prison administration
Tyurémskayi zhízni	Prison life
Tyurémskih styén	(the) Prison walls
Tyurémskiyi srök	(the) Prison sentence
Tyurémskuyu súku	(a) Prison bitch
Tyurémskuyu zhízn	Prison life
Valkóm	Wolf
Vará v zakóne	Thief in law
Var'í v zakóne	Thieves in law
Varóv	Thieves
Varóv v zakóne	Thieves in law
V d'írye	In a hole (segregation block)
Vinó	Wine
Vkusniátina!	Delicious!
Volk	Wolf
Vor	Thief

Vor v zakóne	Thief in law (or in other words, zek/convict who dedicates his life to the criminal life)
Voz'mí sibyá vrúki	Get yourself together
V mayéyi zhízni	In my life
Vranyó	Lies
Vsyó v zhízni	Everything in life
Vrachá	(a) Doctor
Vstáriyi izbyé	In an old log cabin
V temnatyé	In the dark
V tyurémskayi palítiki	In prison politics
V tyúr'mah	In prisons
V tyur'-mé -mú	In prison
V zhízne	In life
Yad	(a) Poison
Ya *óchen'* tabóyi garzhús'!	I am very proud of you!
Ya paterial rázum	I lost my mind
Ya pónil	I understood
Ya lyublyú	I love
Ya nekagdá v prablémye s zakónam nyé bil	I've never been in trouble with the law
Zaffu	Meditation pillow
Zdaróva!	Hello!
Zek	Convict/Con/Prisoner
Zé-kav -kami -ki	Convicts/Cons/Prisoners
Zékav zhivími	Prisoners alive
Zen	Meditation
Zendo	A large meditation hall
Zhénshin	Women
Zhiváya	Alive
Zhiví-m -me	Alive
Zhivóyi	Alive
Zhí-zn -zni	Life
Zhízn v evó glazáh apyát'	The life in his eyes once again
Zhízn v górade	Life in the city
Zhízn v tyur'mé	Life in prison
Zhízn vará	Life of a thief

ZEK

Zhízni yí smérti	Life and death
Zhópu	Ass
Zláya asá	(an) Angry wasp
Zmiyú	Snake
Zver'	(the) Beast
Zveryéyi	Animals

ACKNOWLEDGEMENTS

A special thank you to Ronald Leftwich for editing, to Timothy Miller, Jeff Sinnot, Wayne Grant, James Martin, Nathan Rivera (the author of "In The Image & Likeness"), and Amos Don (the author of "Love Through My Eyes") for their constructive criticism, and to Rodney Ball for his help with the artwork.

Thank you all for your help and support!

www.ingramcontent.com/pod-product-compliance
Lightning Source LLC
Chambersburg PA
CBHW071958070526
44583CB00015B/1245